Marijuana Indoors
Five Easy Gardens

By Jorge Cervantes

D1403263

Published by VPP
Cover Design: Chris Thompson
Artwork: R. Nightengale, Cheeba Grafics
                       Laura Bagliani
Book Design: Chris Thompson
Cover Photo: Jorge Cervantes
Back Cover Photos: Jorge Cervantes
Color Section Photos: Jorge Cervantes
Editors: Annie Riecken
                       Chris Thompson
                       Glenn Curtis
                       Soledad Coyote

Copyright 1999, Jorge Cervantes
ISBN 1-878823-27-2
First Printing
9 8 7 6 5 4 3 2 1

The material in this book is presented as information which should be available to the public. The publisher does not advocate breaking the law.

Neither the publisher nor the authors endorse any products or brand names that are mentioned or pictured in the text. These products are pictured or mentioned for illustration only.

Distributed by: **Marlin's Books**
                19741 41st Ave., NE
                Seattle, WA 98155
                Tel. 1 (888) 306-7187 Orders
                Tel. 1 (206) 306-7187 Questions
                Fax. 1 (206) 306-7188

This book is dedicated to Sebastian Orfali (1946 - 1997)
a great publisher who opened many minds.

Thomas James Lowe
Crohn's Disease Patient
Age 49, sentenced to 8 years, 3 months.
Charged with marijuana cultivation, aiding & abetting.

T.J. Lowe is a photographer and naturopathic physician who studied with the world famous herbologist/iridologist, Bernard Jensen. He used herbs and plants to treat his own Crohn's Disease and to heal others. A doctor at a VA hospital in San Diego recommended *cannabis* along with licorice root extract and ginseng to relieve his cramps, nausea and loss of appetite. T.J. began growing marijuana for himself and AIDS, MS and glaucoma patients, then helped set up three other indoor growing systems. In 1993, the gardens were discovered. T.J. was arrested and charged under federal law.

Although his federal defender assured him he would be given four years if he pled guilty, he was sentenced to 87 months. Soon afterwards, he was beaten by gang members who broke his nose, then confined to 'the hole' for 60 days - a maximum security solitary lockdown isolation cell. T.J. was transferred to Lompoc where he collapsed and required emergency surgery at Valley Center Hospital for an intestinal obstruction from the Crohn's

Disease. Since this was not a prison facility, he was shackled and chained to a bed for 30 days, guarded by armed guards. The surgeon recommended a second operation to remove 12 inches of colon, due to the danger of a rupture, severe diverticuli, and a mass found during the first procedure. Instead, he was transferred to a Federal Medical Center in Texas to save money, where doctors refused to operate. They gave him drugs which caused liver damage, then took him off those drugs, but now refuse to give him medication for nausea and cramps to prevent further damage.

Without proper medical attention, T.J. is condemned to needless suffering. In prison, T.J. returned to *cannabis* to relieve his symptoms. In late 1997 he failed a drug test and was sent back to the hole. In 1998, it happened again. After his release in 1999, T.J. faces five years of supervised release. If a drug test shows marijuana, he goes back to prison. T.J. hopes to benefit from California's Prop 215, which allows medical marijuana with a doctor's recommendation. Since he was charged under federal law, which does not respect a patient's right to use medical marijuana, it is doubtful that he will be allowed to use it.

T.J. needs support and would love to hear from you. You can write to him at:

T.J. Lowe #36414198, 3150 Horton Rd. FTD, Fort Worth, TX 76119.

Shattered Lives: Portraits From America's Drug War, (c) 1998 by Mikki Norris, Chris Conrad and Virginia Resner.

An unflinching look at the people and the human rights violations committed under the auspices of U.S. drug policy. Pictures, stories and analysis based on the internationally ac-claimed photo exhibit, Human Rights and the Drug War.

ISBN 0-9639754-3-9 - 1998 Paperback. 8-1/2 x 11". Color cover, 128 pp, some color. $19.95, plus $3.95 shipping

Check out their website <www.hr95.org>.

Table of Contents

Introduction

Marijuana Indoors: Five Easy Gardens is in response to the Renaissance in marijuana cultivation and *cannabis* culture. There are so many different easy ways to grow marijuana indoors and so many people growing, I thought their stories would be interesting reading. This is not a guide to grow marijuana; it is actual information collected from growers about what they are doing today.

The information contained in this book is derived from personal interviews with hundreds of marijuana growers in North America, Continental Europe, Great Britain and Australia and photographing their gardens.

Each of five case studies explains the course a grower followed beginning to end. Case studies begin with "Growing Statistics", a quick overview of the yield, cost and watts required to set up a garden. An introduction to each case study is next, followed by "Setting Up the Grow Room, Step-by-Step". Next you will see how growers cultivate, maintain, harvest and dry outstanding crops. Yield figures are also included. Excellent information on cloning, cultivation techniques and pest control are also covered in detail.

Growers set up an indoor environment that has everything plants need to grow: light, air, nutrients, growing medium and heat. Light is supplied by high intensity lighting. Air is changed in the room with a vent fan and circulated with an oscillating fan. Nutrients are applied to roots via a nutrient solution anchored in a growing medium. Heat is regulated by a thermostat.

Security and secrecy help successful indoor marijuana growers provide a safe, nurturing environment for their plants to grow. Security and secrecy go hand in hand. The security checklist below outlines many of the growers concerns.

Many growers were interviewed and not profiled. A quick overview of the things that need to change to downsize the garden is included at the end of the chapter. This information essentially shows readers smaller gardens of the growers that were also interviewed. For example, Lee's Closet garden uses 900 watts to grow 1-1/2 pounds in 8 weeks. A similar smaller garden would use 550 watts (one 400-watt and one 150-watt HP sodiums) to grow less dope in the same space. Everything except the number of plants would remain the same.

Chapters end with a list of all the supplies and expenses the grower used to construct the room. There is also a garden calendar that lists all the important dates for each garden. The cost of electricity per crop and per month is also included.

All cost figures are given in 1998 US dollars.

Security Checklist:

1. Electric bill – is it the same as the previous tenants?
2. Outside of the home – does it look similar to other homes in the neighborhood?
3. Light leaks – can light be seen outside the home?
4. Followed home from grow store?
5. Noise – can you hear the fan or ballast from outside the house?
6. Smell – does the crop smell outdoors?

Foreword

Just the Facts

Law enforcement benefits by perpetuating misinformation about marijuana. Law enforcement also vilifies growers by making them into larger-than-life, high-tech bad guys. The bigger and badder their adversary, the better they look. The principle is simple: law enforcement spoon feeds the media to make themselves appear as heroes when they arrest low-life dope growers that are making millions as parasites of society. Dope growers are not only given credit for sky high yields, they are also blamed for many of society's problems!

According to law enforcement officials, each indoor plant produces a pound or more. I recently heard of a legal case where the prosecution claimed the grower on trial was capable of producing nine ounces per square foot of garden space per crop. The grower in question was arrested in possession of 600 clones. This means that if the grower harvested a crop in a 10 x 10-foot room (100 square feet), he should harvest 900 ounces per crop (9 oz. x 100 sq. ft. = 900 oz). 900 ounces divided by 16 ounces equals 56-1/4 pounds! If the grower sold only 50 pounds there would be a profit of $200,000! (50 pounds x $4000 = $200,000). Would you trust a prosecuting attorney that believed that a 100 square foot grow room could produce 56-1/4 pounds? Millions of people put their trust in misinformed prosecuting attorney's just like this one every day.

Growers also perpetuate much misinformation about their actual yield of dry manicured buds. Many growers tend to exaggerate their indoor harvest. One common embellishment some growers claim is that *all* of the plants in a garden are a specific weight. For example, 100 plants are harvested, 60 plants weigh two ounces and 40 weigh an ounce or less. The grower calculates the harvest on the *entire* number of plants that *should* weigh two ounces each. The truly sad part of this common embellishment is that the grower tells this story long enough to enough people that they believe the story to be true. The story becomes more true when the grower retires . . . "You should have seen the crop I grew the winter of '98! The buds were as big as donkey dicks. I never had a crop like it since, I grew four pounds a light . . . it's all gone up in smoke!"

Comparing buds and bunk is another detail to iron out. Growers need a consistent way to measure yield indoors. One grower may claim two pounds per light and another grower claims three ounces per plant, yet another brags about six pounds per table. How much did one grower produce in relation to the other? When three different measurement systems are used, you might as well compare buds and bunk!

Harvest weight is defined using the same two variables: *watts* and *time* to achieve *weight*. A grower's skill is determined by the weight produced of a specific variety. *Watts* and *time* are the limiting factors to achieve *weight*. A grower can alter *watts* by making them provide the absolute most efficient spectrum and volume of light for the garden. *Time* is altered by harvesting as many crops as possible in the shortest time to increase yield. Alter *watts* and *time* properly to achieve maximum harvest *weight*.

There are numerous other variables: fertilizer, soil or hydroponics, HP sodium versus metal halide, square feet of growing space, climate, perpetual yield, sea of green growing technique, etc. are all factors that influence yield. Except for the variety grown, *watts* and *time* are the two limiting factors to produce a heavy harvest. This is why I chose these common denominators among growers to determine yield and their success rate.

Harvest yield is measured in "pounds of dried buds per 1000 watts in the flowering room per 30 days". This means that a two-pound crop grown under a 1000-watt lamp for 60 days produces "one pound per 1000-watts per 30 days". Another example is: one 1000-watt lamp that yields one pound in 60 days of flowering produces 1/2 pound per 1000 watts per 30 days". Grams per watt per 30 days is an easy conversion – 454 grams (one pound) per 1000 watts per month. For example, a 1000-watt lamp that produces 500 grams in a half month, yields one gram per watt.

No allowance is made for cloning or vegetative growth time. Clones easily root in 2 – 3 weeks. Rooted clones grow into strong healthy 12-inch tall vegetative plants in 2 – 3 weeks. A good grower can easily grow bushy clones up to 18 inches tall in less time than it takes for the crop in the 12-hour room to flower.

To learn more about how growers alter *watts* and *time* to maximize *weight*, read on!

Chapter One

Lee's Closet Garden

Growing Statistics:

Yield:	*1 1/2 pounds in 8 weeks*
Cost:	*1st crop: $1667 ($69 per ounce)*
	2nd crop: $200 ($8.30 per ounce)
Space:	*3 x 4 x 8-foot closet*
Watts:	*900*

Lee's Closet Garden

Growing marijuana in pots full of soil is simple and easy. The experienced successful closet grower profiled here uses simple methods that are very easy to follow. I first met Lee at the Chinese restaurant his uncle owns. Lee came to the New World seven years ago to work in his uncle's restaurant and tend the market garden. After learning the ropes in this new land and developing a taste for top quality smoke, Lee decided to put years of Chinese garden knowhow to work. First you will see how he converts a closet into two grow rooms. Next he plants, grows and harvests outstanding buds with a minimum of effort. First time growers love this easy growing example. One grower recently remarked: "I followed Lee's example and grew a great crop the first time. I grew a heavy *indica* cross called 'Shiskeberry' and harvested more than a pound from one 600-watt light over an 8-week crop of clones."

"I growing indoors long time. I use soil and three-gallon bags. I harvest heavy crop very easy," affirmed Lee with a big smile from ear to ear.

"Clones flower fast in three-gallon bags. They easy to grow and no problems," he continued.

Lee uses the single most efficient HID available, the 600-watt HP sodium with an efficient horizontal reflective hood. Chapter Six illuminates the facts of light and shows you why Lee chose the 600-watt HP sodium lamp.

Setting Up the Closet Grow Room: Step-by-Step

The closet grow room is in a 3 x 4 x 8-foot bedroom closet. The vegetative/mother/cloning room is on the ground level and the flowering room built 3-1/2 feet above. The grow room is in Lee's bedroom closet. The bathroom down the hall serves as a work area for transplanting and maintenance.

Two compact grow rooms in a limited space require precision planning. There is little area for light systems and grow containers and every square inch of space, vertical and horizontal, is valuable. Keeping the rooms spotless diminishes insect and fungus problems. There is no room for rubbish in the closet grow room. If it does not promote plant growth, it must hinder plant growth, and Lee removes it from the grow room.

Step One: Lee bought a gallon of quality semigloss white latex paint and painted the entire closet, walls, ceiling and inside the door. He spent $25 to buy *quality* paint and only needed to apply one coat. He covered the floor with two layers of 6-mil plastic and stapled the perimeter to the baseboard. He inserted the staples around the top of the base board so the water would never reach the staple holes and leak. The plastic runs a few inches up the walls so as to catch excess runoff irrigation water.

Step Two: He framed 2 x 4s, 3-1/2 feet from the floor around the walls of the room. He secured the 2 x 4's to the plaster wall using butterfly screws inserted through predrilled holes in the 2 x 4s and walls. Next he cut a 3 x 4-foot piece of 3/4" plywood with a 6 x 6-inch piece cut from the right rear corner for the duct vent. He set the plywood on the 2 x 4 ledge with the vent hole toward the back wall on the right.

He lined the shelf with heavy plastic and made a lip around the wall. Lee secured the plastic to the wall with duct tape.

The plywood shelf formed a partition between the top and bottom of the room. The bottom half of the closet will be the mother/clone/vegetative room and the top half of the closet will be the flowering room.

Step Three: Lee cut a 6-inch and an 8-inch hole in the ceiling of the closet. The holes went through the ceiling and into the attic of the house. He installed a rigid 6-inch stove duct pipe that ran from the ceiling of the bottom room, through the flowering room and ceiling, into the attic. He made the duct by assembling several sections of stovepipe inside the closet. He secured the seams between the sections with duct tape. He blocked off light from the vegetative room around the duct with a few pieces of duct tape. Lee used small screws to attach a 6-inch axial fan at each end of the duct to direct the air up and out of the bottom room.

Lee bought an 18-inch section of 8-inch duct and secured an 8-inch axial fan inside the middle of the duct. Next, he placed the duct and fan securely into the 8-inch hole in the ceiling. The duct was flush against the ceiling to allow all hot air to evacuate up into the attic.

Lee loves axial fans because they are quiet and move air very efficiently when properly installed. He puts them on a rheostat

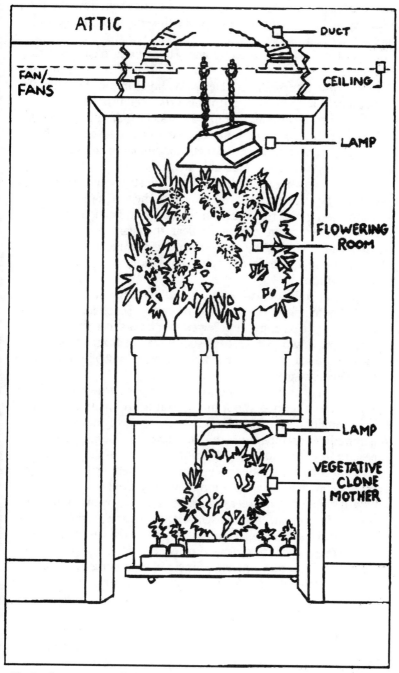

ATTIC

FAN/
FANS

DUCT

CEILING

LAMP

FLOWERING
ROOM

LAMP

VEGETATIVE
CLONE
MOTHER

All the hot air from this closet grow room is vented through the ceiling. The vegetative/clone/mother room is below and the flowering room is above.

(fader switch) to control their speed. He turns them down to the point they make virtually no noise and still keep the room a cool 75 degrees F. 24 hours a day.

Step Four: To install the 600-watt HP sodium in the flowering room, he fastened a 3' x 4' piece of sheet metal 1/2-inch from the ceiling to protect it from heat. He drilled holes in the sheet metal and fastened it to the ceiling with sheet rock screws. Lee also predrilled holes in the ceiling for two hooks he inserted to mount the 600-watt HPS hood and bulb. The remote ballast sits on the nearby shelf. He set up a 600-watt HP sodium lamp and suspended it from two hooks and an adjustable chain.

There was nowhere to keep the HID ballasts except in the closet grow room. Lee made a shelf one foot from the top of the flowering room and set the two 150-watt and the 600-watt ballasts on the shelf. When they begin to generate heat, the nearby vent fans evacuate the hot air quickly. With the extra heat generated by the ballasts in the small closet, adequate ventilation became a matter of success or failure.

Step Five: To install two 150-watt HP sodium lamps in the vegetative room below, Lee first fastened a piece of sheet metal to the vegetative room's ceiling. He screwed four hooks into the lower ceiling and hung two 150-watt HP sodium lamps from adjustable chains from hooks. He hung the fixtures on an angle in the corners to save growing space.

Step Six: Lee installed a thermometer in each grow room. He did not install a thermostat nor humidistat to automatically control the environment because he checks the garden every day and can tell if the humidity or temperature are out of whack. He regulates the temperature and humidity by adjusting the speed of the vent fans with the rheostat. Lee relies on personally inspecting his plants to dictate how much extra ventilation they need. He likes to keep the temperature about 75 degrees F. and the humidity below 50 percent.

Step Seven: Small clip-on oscillating fans come in very handy to circulate air in the closet grow rooms when the door is closed. They are easy to move and direct air where needed. Foliage is packed in tightly during flowering and extra air circulation helps keep bud mold from forming during the last two weeks before harvest.

Lee now has a 900-watt closet grow room that he set up in less than a day.

Step Eight: To totally neutralize the smell of marijuana in the house Lee placed a small container of Ona in his bedroom by the door. He put another container of Ona in the living room and one by the front door of the house. Lee uses Ona to deodorize his grow room because it actually bonds atomically with the smelly marijuana to neutralize the odor.

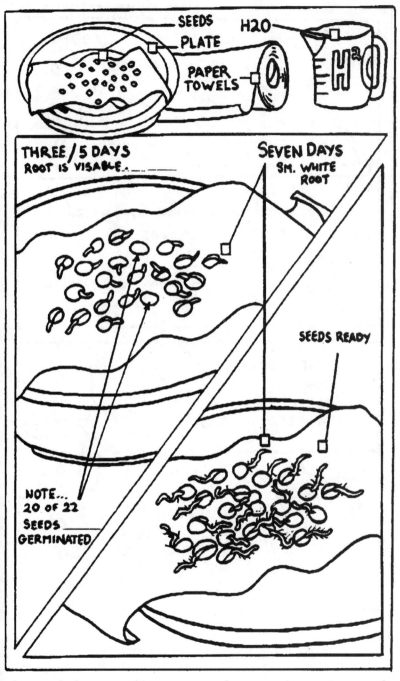

Place seeds between moist paper towels to germinate. In several days, the seeds germinate, growing a small white root. At the end of a week most seeds germinate.

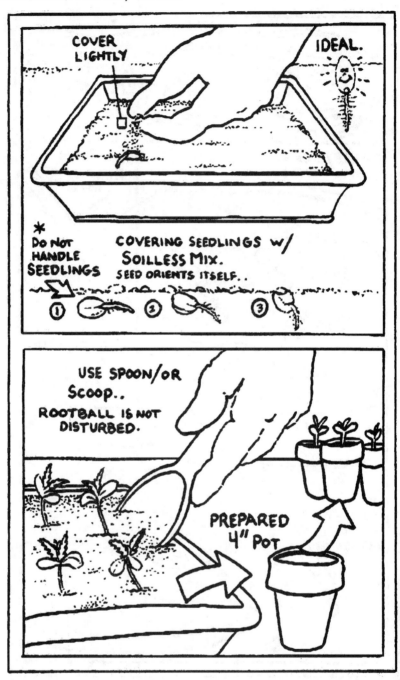

Upper Panel: Cover germinated seeds with fine soilless mix.
Lower Panel: To transplant from the flat, carefully scoop up the root ball with a tablespoon.

Once the room was set up and operational, Lee was ready to germinate the seeds. He followed simple directions from Marc Emery Direct Seed Company in Vancouver, BC, Canada.

Germinating/Planting Seeds

Step One: Lee had 22 seeds that he purchased from one of the seed companies. He had 11 'Northern Lights #5' seeds and 11 'Skunk #1' seeds. He presoaked the seeds in a cup of water for 24 hours.

Step Two: (Day 1) Lee set three paper towels on a dinner plate and poured water on them until they were saturated. He poured the water out of the cup and placed the seeds on the moist paper towels and added three more paper towels to cover the seeds. He drained off all excess water and put the plate on the warm top of his refrigerator. Lee checked the seeds and paper towels daily. He added water if they were dry. The paper towels were kept moist and not soggy.

Step Three: (Day 7) Lee prepared a seed flat for planting. He filled a 10 x 20 x 2-inch flat with a fine 50/50 mix of perlite and peat moss. He watered the mix in the flat with plain water until it was thoroughly saturated and water ran freely from the drainage holes in the bottom. Then he carefully removed each seed and set it on it's side in the flat of soilless seed mix and covered them with ˇ inch layer of moist mix. He spaced seeds 2-3 inches apart. Lee set the seedling flat in the bottom room under one of the 150-watt HP sodium lamps and turned it on.

In four days, 18 of the 20 seeds had broken through the soil and were growing cotyledon leaves. By the end of the week, there were 18 strong seedlings with their first set of true leaves. The other two seedlings grew poorly and were culled out.

Lee watered the seedlings with one-fourth strength Miracle Grow as needed to keep the soil evenly moist.

Transplanting

(Day 14) Lee carefully removed the 18 seedlings and transplanted them into 4-inch pots. He moved the plants back into the vegetative room and turned on both 150-watt HP sodium lamps 18 hours a day. Lee watered the seedlings as needed with one-fourth strength Miracle Grow every other watering to keep the soil moist but not soggy.

(Day 45) The 18 little seedlings grew into strong and healthy plants after a month in the 4-inch pots. Now the plants were 6 weeks old, bushy and 12 to 14 inches tall.

Transplanting is as easy as one, two, three.

To repot them into three-gallon grow bags full of soil, Lee watered the 4-inch pots until water freely flowed from the drain holes. Next, he filled the three-gallon bags half full of coarse potting soil and saturated them with water. Then he again watered the seedlings in 4-inch pots. He let them stand long enough to smoke two joints.

Lee carefully turned each 4-inch pot upside down and tenderly shook the intact root ball into his hand. Lee carefully placed the root ball on the soil in the three-gallon pot. He gingerly packed more potting soil around the wet root ball. He watered the transplanted seedling heavily with a fertilizer solution containing vitamin B^1, which eased transplant shock. Once the first seedling was transplanted and watered, Lee moved to the next seedling. Soon the shower was full with 18 foot-tall seedlings in three-gallon grow bags.

Flowering

(**Day 45**) When all the seedlings were transplanted, Lee set them in the flowering room under 12 hours of 600-watt HP sodium light. The 18 three-gallon pots packed the 3 x 4-foot flowering room wall to wall.

Lee watered the transplants only twice during the first two weeks. By the third week they had grown so big that they required water every 2 – 3 days. Lee watered the plants as needed so the soil was moist, but not soggy. He fertilized with a hydroponic flowering formula every second watering.

Lee uses a two-gallon water can with a spout to reach and water plants. The spout has a sprinkler/breaker that adds air to the nutrient solution just before it enters the soil. Keeping the plants watered evenly is Lee's biggest challenge.

(**Day 60**) The plants showed signs of flowering during the second and third weeks under 12 hours of light. Male plants were easy to spot and remove over the two-week period. At the end of the culling process there were 10 female plants. Lee had beaten the odds. Normally 50 percent of the plants are male and 50 percent female (see male and female plants in color section). Lee removed

---

Lee could . . .

take three clones from each female plant and root them in a flat of rooting mix under 18 hours of light from a 150-watt HP sodium lamp. See instructions on cloning in Chapter Five.

Flush excess fertilizer (salt build-up) from pots every month. Flush pots with at least two gallons of water for each gallon of soil.

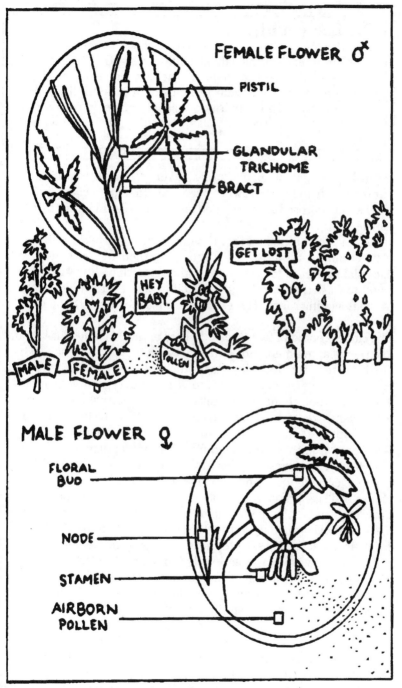

Female plants (top) grow a pair of white pistils from seed bracts.
Male plants (bottom) grow a pod that sheds pollen.

OR Lee could . . .

grow the young plants for three more weeks before taking two clones from each plant, labeling the clone and corresponding parent plant. Then Lee could set the new clones in the closet cloning room and give them 12 hours of fluorescent light. The little clones will show their sex, male or female, in two weeks. He will cull out all the male plants when the clones show their sex.

the male plants before pollen sacks had fully formed. He carefully put the plants in his microwave oven and dried them enough to smoke. This procedure also killed any pollen that might fertilize his female crop.

At the end of the first month of flowering, Lee takes all the plants from the flowering room and places them in the shower. He uses plain water in his water can and gives each plant 4 gallons of water to wash away any fertilizer buildup before returning the plants to the flowering room. He resumes normal feeding with the next watering.

The clones rooted in two weeks. Twenty of the 36 clones thrived and Lee transplanted them into 4-inch pots of coarse potting soil. The clones were in the flowering stage when taken; they had to grow roots and revert from flowering growth back to vegetative growth. The clones took about three weeks to resume normal growth. All weak plants were culled out and never moved to the flowering room. He transplanted the strongest clones into three-gallon grow bags five weeks after they were taken from the mother plants.

He cloned a few strong healthy females and set them in the vegetative/clone room under the HP sodium light. In two weeks the clones had strong roots. He potted the rooted clones in one-gallon grow bags and let them grow under 18 hours of light for two weeks. Then he moved them up to the flowering room to finish flowering for 8 more weeks. He set a few more clones up in the flowering room every few days. Staggering their move to the flowering room also staggered the harvest. Lee also chose several different varieties such as 'Skunk #1' (10 weeks) and 'Romulan' (8 weeks) and 'Haze' (12+ weeks) that mature at different times. 'Romulan' topped out at 24-inches-tall and 'Skunk #1' was 3-feet-tall at harvest. All of the tall plants had to be bent to keep from touching the light.

Removing the male plants keeps them from fertilizing their female counterparts. Unfertilized female marijuana flower buds, called *sinsemilla* – Spanish for "without seeds", is more resin-packed and potent than seeded flower buds. Male plants are even less potent than seeded flower buds.

White female pistils stretching from unpollinated female flowers became increasingly prominent every day flowering progressed (see 8-page color section). By the end of the fifth week, buds began to swell and resin glands were forming everywhere on the buds.

(Day 90) Large older leaves began to yellow the sixth week because Lee had completely stopped fertilizing. The flowering females received only plain water during the last two weeks before harvest. Irrigating with plain water washes away the fertilizer taste from the dried buds.

Lee is very careful not to overfertilize his crop. The coarse potting soil already has fertilizer added and it is easy to overfertilize. For more information on overfertilization, see Chapter Two.

Spider mites also made an appearance in the closet garden. Because he visits his garden daily, Lee was quick to notice them and to act. He turned off the vent fans and fogged both rooms with pyrethrum in an aerosol can. Two of the brand names of the aerosol with pyrethrum as the active ingredient include: Pokon and Widmire's Exclude. He cracked the door open and sprayed the room heavily with the aerosol for several minutes. Lee was careful to keep the nozzle at least one foot away from tender plants. The spray comes out of the nozzle at sub zero temperatures and takes about a foot to warm up enough so that foliage is not damaged.

Lee repeated the spray with pyrethrum in an aerosol can two more times at seven-day intervals. Fogging the entire room heavily ensures spray gets under leaves to kill mites and eggs.

He leaves the door of the closet garden open whenever the flowering light is on. The added ventilation helps plants grow better and stay healthy.

Harvest

(Day 105) Lee inspected the resin glands on the female buds with a 30X microscope every day during the 8th week to discern peak ripeness. He picked one of the plants the beginning of the 8th week and dried enough to smoke for a week in the microwave oven. To dry in the microwave, Lee cut the moist buds into small pieces. He put the bud in the microwave on full power. He checked the bud every 10 seconds to see if it was dry enough to smoke. He harvested 14 plants the first day of the 9th week and let the last three plants grow until the end of the 9th week.

He harvested from 1 to 2 ounces per plant depending on how much light the plant received.

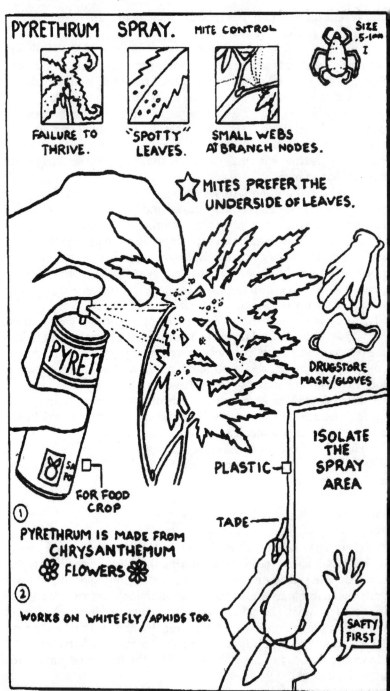

Natural pyrethrum fogged from an aerosol kills mites where they live on leaf undersides.

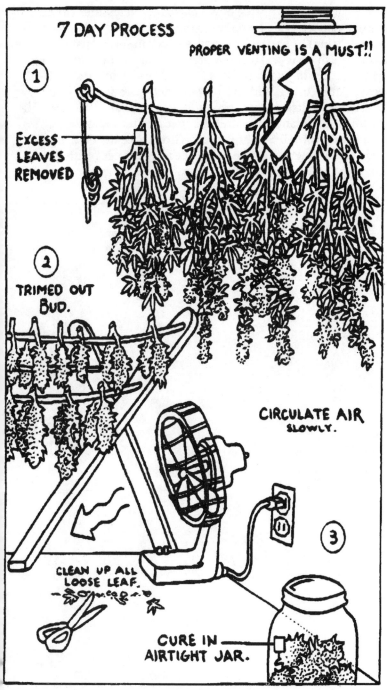

Growers dry harvested plants by hanging from a line. Good air circulation and ventilation ensures buds will dry evenly.

He hangs plants upside down on strings in another closet to dry for a day or two. Then he removes the large leaves and branches before putting the partially manicured buds in several paper grocery bags to finish drying. The buds are smokable in 4 to 7 days. Once dry, Lee places his stash in glass jars and lets them cure for 6 – 7 weeks. After curing, buds burn evenly and taste sweet.

Buds are a little looser than those grown under 1000-watt HP sodium bulbs. Plants also stretch between internodes (branches) when exclusively HPS light is used. Grower's that add a metal halide containing more blue in the spectrum notice plants are a bit more compact, but weigh a little less.

Construction Supplies

Approximate Cost

Board, 3/4" plywood – 2' x 3'	$12
Board, 1" x 12" x 3'	$5
Boards, 3, 2" x 4" x 8'	$12
Duct pipe – (6" x 6') (8" x 3')	$45
Duct Tape	$5
Electric drill and drill bits – Lee already owns a drill and bits	$0
Electric circular saw – Lee already owns a circular saw	$0
Fans – 1, 6-inch axial, 2, 8-inch axial, 2, clip-on oscillating	$200
Hardware (hooks, screws, chain, etc.)	$10
Lights – one 600-watt HPS, two 150-watt HPS	$800
Rheostats – 3, one for each vent fan	$30
Plastic for floors – 6 mil x 6' x 24'	$8
Screws, 12 butterfly	$10
Sheet metal, 2, (3' x' 4') pieces for ceiling heat guard	$10
Stapler – borrowed from friend + staples	$5
Thermometers, one for each room	$20
Timers for lights	$40
White paint, 3-inch paint brush, roller and paint pan	$30

Growing Supplies

Fertilizer – Miracle Gro, B[1], Hydro-flower	$20
Flat – 10" x 20" x 2" seedling flat with drainage	$5
Microscope, 30X	$50
Paper towels – for germination	$2
Pots – 50, 4" pots, 50, 3-gallon grow bags	$30
Pruners	$20
Rooting hormone jell	$10
Seeds: Northern Lights #5 and Skunk #1	$300
Soil 4 cubic	$30
Spray, Pokon miticide (pyrethrum)	$10
Water can – 2-gallon	$10

Total $1729.00

Electricity

(also see chart in Appendix)

600-watts (0.6) x 12 hrs x 30 days = 216 kilowatt-hours (KWH)

300-watts (0.3) x 24 hrs x 30 days = 216 kilowatt-hours

216 + 216 = 432 kilowatt hours per month

432 x $0.10 (cost of KWH) = **$43.20** increase in monthly electricity bill if electricity costs $0.10 per KWH.

Running the vegetative/clone room 18 hours a day would save about $5 in electricity per month.

$1729 Setup Cost +

$43.20 - 30-day electricity bill

$43.20 - 30-day electricity bill

= $1815.40 Total cost to grow first crop

$1815/24 ounces = **$76** per ounce for the first crop

$200/24 ounces = **$8.30** per ounce for each additional crop

Garden Calendar

1.	Germinate seed	January 1
2.	Plant seed	January 7
3.	Transplant to 4-inch pot	January 14
4.	Transplant to 3-gallon pot	February 14
5.	Induce flowering with 12-hour days	February 14
6.	Change to flowering fertilizer	February 14
7.	Stop fertilizing – feed plain water	April 1
8.	Harvest	April 14
9.	Take clones for sex	March 7
10.	Learn sex, cull males, take female clones	March 21
11.	Transplant clones to 3-gallon pots	April 7
12.	Induce flowering	May 21
13.	Harvest	July 20

Growing Statistics

Yield:	20 ounces every 8 weeks
Lbs/1000-w/30 days:	1.25
Grams/watt/30 days:	0.56
Clone room:	Root 30 clones 14 days
Part of vegetative	two 150-watt HPS
room	24 hours per day
	Fine perlite/peat moss
Vegetative room:	Grow 12 plants for 3 weeks
3 x 4 x 3 ° feet	two 150-watt HPS
	24 hours per day
	three-gallon grow bags of coarse potting soil
Flowering room:	Grow 12 plants for 8 weeks
3 x 4 x 4 feet	One 600-watt HPS
	12 hours per day
	three-gallon grow bags of coarse potting soil
Harvest:	12, 2 – 3-foot tall plants
Average weight	1 – 2 ounces each.

Monthly electricity cost (@ *$0.10 per KWH*)**:** $43.20
First crop cost: $1815.40 total ($76 per ounce)
Next crop cost: $200 ($8.30 per ounce)

• **To downsize his garden by 40 percent,** Lee would use one 400-watt and one 150-watt HP sodium lamp. He would still use the same closet and all of his other construction expenses would be the same. The smaller lights generate less heat and a smaller fan could be installed, but this would not allow for expansion later. Lee's work load and harvest would also decrease by 40 to 50 percent.

Yield: 12 ounces every 8 weeks	
Lbs/1000-w/30 days: 1.2	
Grams/watt/30 days: 0.5	
Clone room:	Root 18 clones 14 days
Part of vegetative	two 150-watt HPS
room	24 hours per day
	Fine perlite/peat moss
Vegetative room:	Grow 8 plants for 3 weeks
	3 x 4 x 3 ° feet two 150-watt HPS
	24 hours per day
	three-gallon grow bags of coarse potting soil
Flowering room:	Grow 8 plants for 8 weeks
3 x 4 x 4 feet	One 600-watt HPS

	12 hours per day
	three-gallon grow bags of coarse potting soil
Harvest:	12, 2 – 3-foot tall plants
	Average weight 1 – 1-1/2 ounces each.

Monthly electricity cost: (@ $0.10 per KWH): $21.00
First crop cost: $1467 total ($125 per ounce)
Next crop cost: $70 ($5.80 per ounce)

• **To downsize his garden by 80 percent,** Lee would use one 150-watt HP sodium lamp and two 40-watt fluorescent tubes. He would still use the same closet and all of his other construction expenses would be the same. The smaller lights generate less heat and a smaller fan could be installed, but this would not allow for expansion later. Lees work load and harvest would also decrease more than 75 percent.

Yield: 3.2 ounces every 8 weeks
Lbs/1000-w/30 days: 1
Grams/watt/30 days: 0.45

Clone room:	Root 8 clones 14 days
Part of vegetative	two 150-watt HPS
room	24 hours per day
	Fine perlite/peat moss
Vegetative room:	Grow 4 plants for 3 weeks
3 x 4 x 3-1/2 feet	two 150-watt HPS
	24 hours per day
	three-gallon grow bags of coarse potting soil
Flowering room:	Grow 4 plants for 8 weeks
3 x 4 x 4 feet	One 600-watt HPS
	12 hours per day
	three-gallon grow bags of coarse potting soil
Harvest:	12, 2 – 2-1/2-foot tall plants
	Average weight 1+ ounces each.

Monthly electricity cost (@ $0.10 per KWH): $8.00
First crop cost: $749 total ($234.00 per ounce)
Next crop cost: $250 ($7.81 per ounce)

Chapter Two
'Romulan' Joe's Garden

Growing Statistics:

Yield:	*2 pounds in 8 weeks*
Cost:	*1st crop: $2600 ($72.20 per ounce)*
	2nd crop: $300 ($8.30 per ounce)
Space:	*10 x 15 feet*
Watts:	*1760*

'Romulan' Joe's Garden

"Romulan' Joe" grew up in a family that owned a nursery in Southern California. He worked in the family nursery from childhood until he graduated from college. Now he lives in a Midwest city and works in the hotel industry.

Joe's garden techniques are easy and virtually foolproof. First you will see how he constructs a simple grow room from the ground up. Then Joe plants, grows and harvests great marijuana with ease.

"I've been growing indoors for 15 years . . . might say it's in my blood. I must have used or seen about every kind of growing system. A lot of hydroponic systems work, we used to grow hydroponically back home. But I'll tell you complex hydroponic systems are unforgiving and too much can go wrong. I grow hydroponically in 6-liter pails full of coarse soilless mix. The soilless mix I use is called Sunshine #4*. It is peat moss, perlite, dolomite lime and a complete range of soluble nutrients (fertilizer) impregnated into the mix. I think some sort of similar coarse soilless mix is available everywhere," said 'Romulan' Joe as he passed me a huge spliff.

* Sunshine #1 and Sunshine #4 are commercial soilless potting mixes available in Northwestern North America. Many nurseries carry similar soilless mixes. Sunshine #4 is a coarse mix of peat moss, perlite, dolomite lime, nutrients and a wetting agent. Sunshine #1 is a finer mix for seedlings containing nutrients and a wetting agent. Marijuana flourishes in a coarse soilless mix that provides plenty of space for air, nutrient solution and roots. Fertilizer levels in soilless mix are easy to control. Fertilizer can be easily added or flushed away.

Setting Up the Grow Room: Step-by-Step

Step One: 'Romulan' Joe cleaned out a 10' x 15' corner of his basement to locate his grow rooms. 'Romulan' Joe went to Home Depot, picked up and read several pamphlets about framing walls and installing pre-hung doors. He also *explained* his project to the sales clerk. He told the clerk he wanted to add a guest room in the basement. The clerk helped him plan the project and gave him many helpful construction hints. Joe purchased all the necessary supplies. He framed in two walls with 2 x 4s and covered the outside with sheet rock. He installed a pre-hung solid-core door with a deadbolt lock he bought at Home Depot. He covered the inside of the room, walls and ceiling with black/white Visqueen plastic. He covered the 2" x 4" stud wall with the plastic using a staple gun.

Step Two: Once the room was in place and totally white inside, he was ready to divide it into separate flowering and vegetative rooms. He hung two pieces of black/white plastic 6 inches apart to divide the rooms. He stapled each piece to the ceiling and duct taped them to the floor with the white side facing out. The 6-inch space between walls prevents light transmission between the two rooms. He also installed an 8-inch duct between the rooms. The air flow between the rooms vents the vegetative grow room. He hung the new plastic walls all the way across the room to split the large room into one 5 x 10-foot vegetative/clone room and one 10 x 10-foot flowering room. 'Romulan' Joe used duct tape to fasten the sides of the walls together and ran another piece of duct tape around the ceiling to secure the Visqueen walls. He cut a door in the plastic walls after they were in place and fastened Velcro around the door. He used duct tape to fasten another piece of overlapping plastic to form a door. The Velcro holds the plastic door closed and the dual wall prevents light from penetrating.

Step Three: Cloning Chamber Construction

'Romulan' Joe framed a small cloning chamber with 2 x 4's and covered it with plastic. The simple drawing shows exactly how to construct the chamber. A list of all the necessary components is included. Dimensions are 2 feet deep, 4 feet tall and 4 feet wide. It is covered with black/white plastic with black on the outside. There is a plywood shelf two feet from the bottom of the chamber. Two 4-foot-long fluorescent tubes are suspended above rooting clones by pulleys on nylon ropes. Joe always predrilled screw holes before he secured the components together using sheet rock screws and a power screwdriver.

Components to manufacture a 2 x 4 x 4-foot cloning chamber.

4 – 1" x 2" x 4'	4 – 2" x 4" x 4'
4 – 1" x 2" x 2'	2 – 1/2" x 2' x 4' plywood

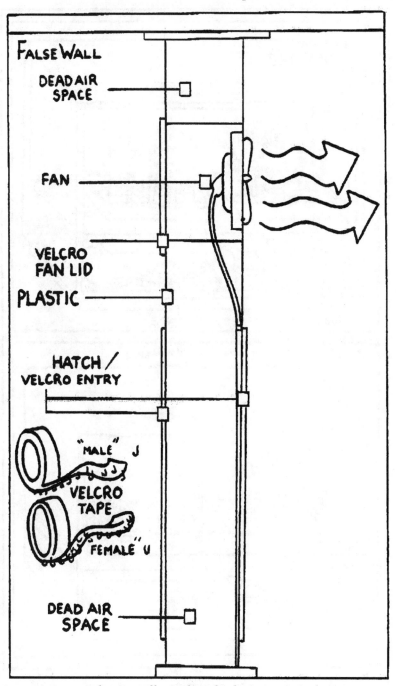

FALSE WALL

DEAD AIR SPACE

FAN

VELCRO FAN LID

PLASTIC

HATCH / VELCRO ENTRY

"MALE" J

VELCRO TAPE

FEMALE" U

DEAD AIR SPACE

Joe set up two plastic walls with a dead air space in between to form a light baffle. Air passes between the rooms and light does not.

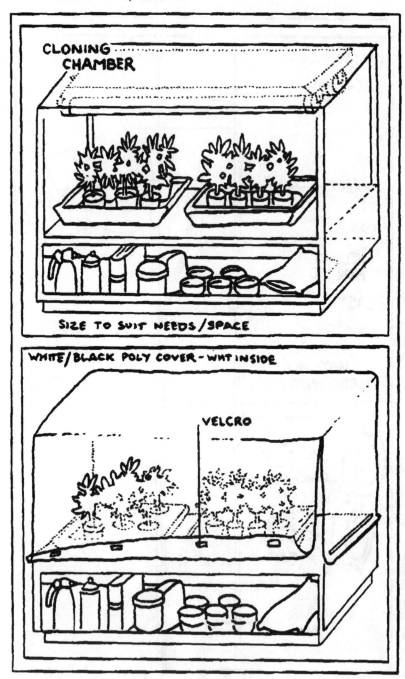

Joe framed this inexpensive cloning chamber with 1 x 2-inch boards, installed a fluorescent fixture, shelf and covered it with plastic in less than two hours.

Step Four: 'Romulan' Joe was ready to install the 800 cubic foot per minute (CFM) squirrel cage blower to vent the room. Noise is not an issue to 'Romulan' Joe because he lives in the country and his two 120-pound Rottweiler guard dogs keep unwanted visitors on the other side of the "NO TRESPASSING" signs. He suspended the vent fan from two eyebolts screwed into the floor joists in the ceiling of his basement grow room. Six inches from the ceiling, 'Romulan' Joe used a utility knife to cut an 8-inch hole through the plastic and sheet rock wall for the duct. He ran flexible 8-inch ducting through the hole and into the nearby chimney of an unused fireplace. He attached the other end of the flexible ducting to the exhaust of the blower with duct tape. Joe kept the ducting straight and smooth so the air flows easily. A small bend, or worst of all, a 90-degree corner, will cut air flow by half or more!

'Romulan' Joe bought a thermostat/humidistat and plugged it into a 120V wall outlet in the flowering room. He plugged the 800 CFM vent fan into the thermostat and set it to turn the fan on when the temperature climbs beyond 75 degrees or humidity rises above 50 percent.

'Romulan' Joe installed a 240 CFM squirrel cage blower in the mother/clone/vegetative room. He suspended the fan from two eye bolts in overhead joists and vented it through the Visqueen plastic wall with 6-inch ducting into the flowering room with a short piece of rigid six-inch ducting. He did not need a timer for this vent fan because he keeps it running 24 hours a day to keep air circulated at night between rooms. Joe set up two, 16-inch oscillating circulation fans at opposite ends of the flowering room. He set up one, 16-inch oscillating circulation fan in the mother/vegetative room.

Now 'Romulan' Joe has two white rooms with climate control. The vent fan controls the temperature and humidity in the room.

Step Five: 'Romulan' Joe did his research on lighting and found the 600-watt HP sodium with the proper horizontal hood the most efficient and absolute best value. He secured a 2 x 4 across the white plastic ceiling of the flowering room at a 30-degree angle with lag bolts screwed into floor joists. Next, he screwed mounting hooks into the 2 x 4 to hang his 600-watt HP sodium lights. He hung the lamps parallel to the 30-degree 2 x 4 so they illuminated a 4 x 8-foot area. He screwed in the hooks five feet from each corner.

He used lengths of chain to hang two 600-watt reflector and bulb fixtures from the hooks. The chain makes it easy to adjust the height of the lamp above the plants. He ran the electrical cords from the lamp along the ceiling and through a hole in the wall to the remote ballasts. 'Romulan' Joe bundled the electrical cords with cable ties to keep them out of the way.

Joe screwed hooks into the ceiling in the mother/vegetative room to mount the 400-watt HP sodium lamp and mounted the fixture with adjustable chain.

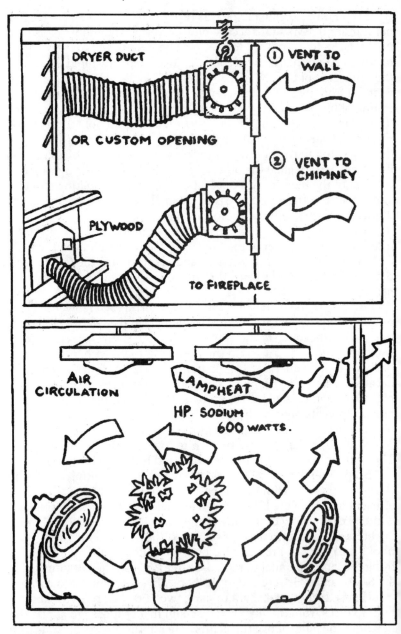

Upper Panel: All grow rooms must have adequate ventilation. Venting out the chimney or through a wall evacuates hot moist air efficiently. To avoid detection, Joe deodorizes the air before expelling.

Lower Panel: An oscillating fan circulates grow room air, reducing stratification and increases water and nutrient consumption.

Joe's room has good lighting, air circulation and ventilation to replicate an outdoor climate.

Step Six: He knocked a hole in the concrete basement floor with a jackhammer to make a drain hole. He installed a sump pump in the drain hole to pump runoff water to the garden outside.

Having a drain made his garden more efficient and easier to manage. It also gave Joe a chance to make a hole in a concrete floor with a jackhammer.

Joe picked an out-of-the-way corner in the grow room floor for the reservoir and drew a two-foot circle on the concrete. He put on his safety goggles, stuffed cotton in his ears, and plugged in the electric jackhammer. Mentally, he went through the instructions the rental clerk had given him earlier that day. The bit tore holes in the concrete as he held the gyrating handles of the jackhammer. Less than ten minutes later, Joe had chiseled out a two-foot round hole in the concrete. He picked up the concrete chunks and put them into a 20-gallon plastic container. He continued to chisel the hard soil and rock below the concrete. After about 45 minutes of chiseling and digging, he managed to make the hole 3 feet deep, just the right size for a 30-gallon reservoir to catch runoff water. Joe uses his 1250 gallon-per-hour (GPH) pump to lift this solution to the outdoor garden.

Before putting in the drain in the floor, Joe had to vacuum up the runoff irrigation water with his heavy duty shop-vac.

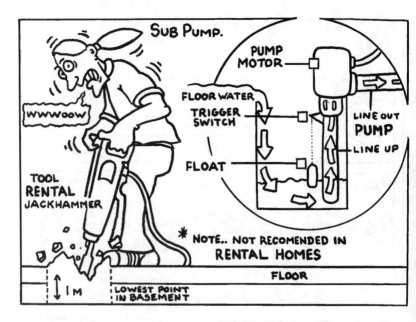

Joe used a jackhammer to make a hole in the basement floor to install a sump pump.

'Romulan' Joe loves to grow and smoke 'Romulan', an Afghani genotype. He has been growing marijuana for many years and settled on this very simple method because it is easy and productive. 'Romulan' Joe realized a long time ago that light was the biggest limiting factor to growing indoors, and did his homework. Check out "Illuminating Facts of Light" in Chapter Six for a summary of his homework and learn why 'Romulan' Joe settled on a 600-watt HP sodium.

'Romulan' is one of the new varieties that came from British Columbia, Canada. The small, tightly packed buds are teeming with THC. "Romulan's' growth habit is short and stout. Resin begins to appear during the last few weeks of flowering. At peak harvest, upon close inspection with a 30X microscope, heavy resin (capitate-stalked trichomes) are everywhere on ripe buds. This plant with a Hindu-Kush growing habit has Afghani heritage and it is a light bud producer.

Taking Clones

(Day 1) 'Romulan' Joe takes clones from a mother plant he keeps under a 400-watt HP sodium lamp in the 5 x 5-foot vegetative room. The mother is kept in a ten-gallon pot full of Sunshine #4. He fertilizes as needed. Before he cuts clones, 'Romulan' Joe fills two 10 x 20-inch nursery flats with Sunshine #1 soilless mix and saturates it with 1/4-strength Nutrilife™ fertilizer. When the soilless mix is saturated and the excess water has drained out the bottom, he uses a pencil to make 25, 1-inch-deep holes in the mix of each flat.

Next, he carefully takes three-inch clones from his mother plant and dips them in Nutrilife™ Rooting Jell before inserting the stem in the pre-made hole. 'Romulan' Joe is careful to keep rooting jell on the stem when putting it in each hole. Once the trays are full with 25 cuttings each, he waters with 1/4-strength Nutrilife™ and packs soil around stems. Clones grow roots much faster when the soil is in firm contact with the stem. See 8-page color section for a complete pictorial sequence on taking clones.

Filling a 5-gallon bucket with a mix of diluted pyrethrum and lemon juice, Joe dips each clone (submerges foliage) in the bucket of miticide before moving it to the flowering room. This keeps spider mites at bay. The lemon juice (10 drops per quart) helps dry out and kill both mites and eggs. The dip completely covers and kills spider mites and their eggs.

Joe sets the two flats of clones in the cloning chamber and adjusts the fluorescent light fixture to 4 inches above the flats. He closes the plastic front. 'Romulan' Joe opens the cloning chamber

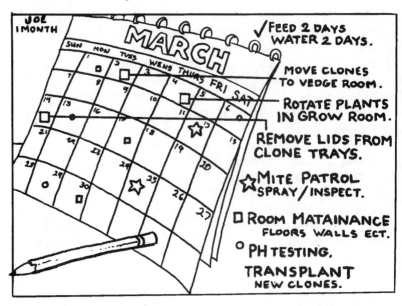

Joe's calendar helps him schedule maintenance and keep the garden producing the maximum. He keeps old calendars at a friends house for added security.

two or three times daily and mists the clones with water. Opening the cloning chamber also allows fresh air circulation. 'Romulan' Joe checks the soil for moisture daily. The soil's surface should remain moist and not soggy. Drainage holes in the bottom of the flat allow water to drain away readily. He waters two to four times, depending on need, during the two week rooting period.

Vegetative Growth

(Day 15) 'Romulan' Joe transplants rooted clones into three-liter pails. He dips them again in diluted pyrethrum and lemon juice before transplanting. The 3-liter clones are given 18 hours of 400-watt HP sodium light for the next three weeks. Now 'Romulan' Joe transplants the foot-tall vegetative clones into 6 liter pails. The clones spend two more weeks in vegetative growth under 18 hours of light.

At first he huddles vegetative plants under one lamp and adds the second 600-watt lamp as plants grow larger and require more light. This keeps his electric use fluctuating up and down and lower overall. A high and consistent electricity bill is one of the tips law enforcement uses to attain a search warrant.

Plants are spaced close together in three-liter pails in the 10 x 10-foot flowering room. 'Romulan' Joe crams about 40 plants into the flowering room. It is standing room only in the flowering forest of 'Romulan'. During the last week before harvest, 'Romulan' Joe has to move some of the plants around in the flowering room to make room for him to water. Moving the plants is an easy job and saves the buds from any damage.

(Day 37) Joe transplants the bushy clones into 6-liter pails after they have been growing in the 3-liter pails for three weeks. The clones in then stay in the vegetative room for two more weeks.

There are 20 flowering females, 30 vegetative clones and two mother plants, a total of 52 plants. 'Romulan' Joe is ready to harvest after 56 days of flowering under 12-hour days/nights. The grower takes clones 7 weeks before the next harvest. Clones root for two weeks and are kept in the vegetative growth stage for 5 more weeks (total 7 weeks from taking cuttings). He harvests 20 female plants, moves the 5-week-old vegetative plants into the flowering room and takes new clones one week later.

Fertilization and Care

'Romulan' Joe uses a watering wand attached to a 1/2-inch hose to reach and water plants. The wand has a water-breaker/sprinkler head that adds air to the nutrient solution just before it enters the container. The other end of the hose is attached to a 1250 GPH pump submerged in a 33-gallon plastic garbage can full of nutrient solution.

To ensure all plants receive enough water and retain no dry soil pockets, he waters heavily, allowing 10 to 20 percent of the water to run out the drain holes in the bottom of the pots. He also cultivates the surface of the soil with his fingers to ensure even water penetration.

According to 'Romulan' Joe, "the biggest problem I have is watering. If I don't take my time at it, the water does not penetrate the soil evenly. All I have to do is remember to pick up the pails. I know how much water is in them by how heavy they are. That's why I always water the hell out of them, I let it run out the holes in the bottom all over the floor. This way I'm sure the soil is wet".

'Romulan' Joe mixes Nutrilife™ (A + B) in a 33-gallon plastic container with a submerged 1250 GPH pump attached to a lightweight 1/2-inch hose. Watering by hand gives him time to look at each plant closely. By checking plants daily, he gets to know each plant and every detail about how it grows.

Joe uses a pump submerged in nutrient solution to irrigate his garden. The water wand with an aerating nozzle adds air to the solution. Joe keeps the pH of the nutrient solution at 6.5 and checks it daily with a pH pen.

'Romulan' Joe is fortunate, because the water that comes out of his tap is very clean. It has a low level of dissolved solids and the pH is 6.8, perfect for growing in soilless mix. When 'Romulan' Joe adds fertilizer to the water, the pH drops to 6. He applies nutrient solution with a pH of 6 to the soilless mix and the pH stays near 6.2 in the soilless mix. 'Romulan' Joe uses an inexpensive electronic pH meter to measure the pH of the nutrient solution and the soilless mix.

He fertilizes every third or fourth watering. 'Romulan' Joe lets 15 - 20 percent drain through the container on the days he applies plain water. The water runs out on the floor and drains into the basement drain hole or evaporates into the air and is carried outdoors via the vent fan. He continues this schedule during five-weeks of vegetative growth.

He flushes the flowering females with two gallons of water per gallon of soil after three weeks of growing. This is done to avert any nutrient buildup problems the day before he is ready to move plants into the flowering room.

Flowering

(Day 51) Clones are 15 to 18 inches tall after five weeks of vegetative growth (after the initial two weeks to grow roots). At this point, 'Romulan' Joe moves clones in 6-liter pails into the flowering room under 12 hours of HP sodium light. Two horizontal 600-watt HP sodium lamps illuminate a 10 x 10-foot growing area. Clones show signs of flower production within two weeks. 'Romulan' clones are ripe 8 weeks (56 days) after flowering is induced.

The fertilizer regimen changes to Nutrilife™ (A + C) when the plants move into the flowering room. 'Romulan' Joe continues to fertilize every 3rd – 4th watering for the next 4 weeks. He also continues to let at least 15 percent of the water drain out the bottom of the containers onto the floor.

(Day 93) The last two weeks before harvest, 'Romulan' Joe stops fertilizing altogether and applies only plain water. The plain water regimen ensures buds will taste sweet and chemical-free. All fertilizer taste is washed away when plants are flushed for two weeks.

Insect, Fungus and Nutrient Problem Solving

After plants are flowering for about three weeks is when problems can set in. To prevent problems, 'Romulan' Joe flushes the

FERTILIZER

Use a complete fertilizer such as a hydroponic fertilizer that has all necessary nutrients in an available form. Soilless mixes have no nutrients unless added by the manufacturer or grower. Growing with soilless mix and applying nutrient solution manually is low-tech hydroponics. 'Romulan' Joe is watering and feeding by hand which takes the place of an automatic irrigation system.

Many soilless mixes are fortified with fertilizer and wetting agent. Be sure to check and see what has been added to any store-bought soilless mix. Stay away from soilless mixes that have time-release fertilizers added. Time-release fertilizers are difficult to control.

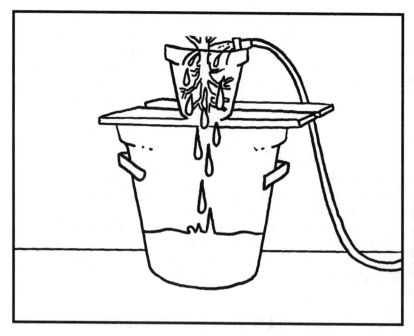

Joe flushes all plants in the garden every month with two gallons of water for each gallon of soilless mix to avoid nutrient problems.

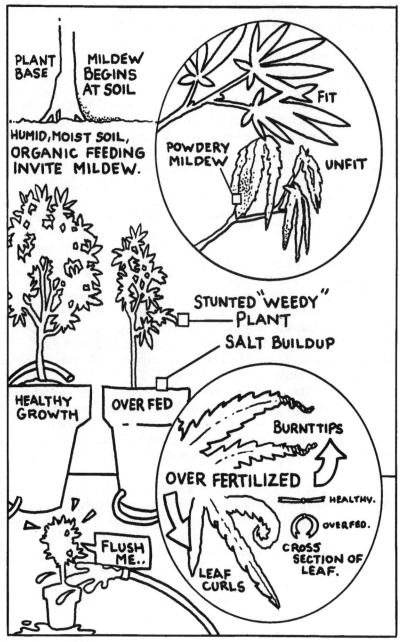

Powdery mildew is avoided by good air circulation and
venting the air out of the room when the humidity climbs beyond
50 percent. Monthly flushing containers with two gallons of
plain water for each gallon of soilless mix will help avoid
overfertilization.

soilless mix heavily. Powdery mildew, spider mites and nutrient lockout can occur the second or third week of flowering. Powdery mildew is easy to spot. It looks like a white powdery substance sprinkled on the leaves.

To stop powdery mildew, 'Romulan' Joe dilutes a tablespoon of baking soda (bicarbonate of soda) per quart of water and applies it directly to the powdery mildewed leaves with a small hand sprayer. The baking soda changes the pH of the leaf surface to seven. Powdery mildew cannot grow in an environment with a pH of seven. Joe sprays as soon as he sees any trace of mildew. He lets the baking soda spray stay on leaves a few hours then he washes it off with plain water. He also increases ventilation and lowers humidity to 40 percent. 'Romulan' Joe sprays only well-rooted, well-watered plants. He does not spray clones. This spray can kill tender clones that are not well-rooted.

Joe rarely has any trouble with mites because he dips entire plants in a miticide, but when they first appear, he sprays with pyrethrum in an aerosol can.

Leaching the 6-liter pails with 12 liters of water solves overfertilization and nutrient lockup problems. Leaves that start to yellow mean that the plant has a nutrient deficiency. This deficiency is caused by nutrients being made unavailable due to excessive fertilizer (salt) buildup or lack of fertilizer in the soilless mix. When some nutrients build up to toxic levels, they make other nutrients unavailable. When the pH of the growing medium is between 6 and 6.5, all the nutrients should be available. Leaching, or pouring two gallons of plain water for each gallon of soilless mix, will flush (leach) out any excessive fertilizer salt buildup. Once the soilless mix is flushed, 'Romulan' Joe waits until the next watering to apply fertilizer.

Leaves that are yellow between the veins have a nitrogen deficiency; there is not enough iron available as a catalyst to make the nitrogen available. The solution to this problem, chlorosis, is to leach pots with two gallons of water for each gallon of soilless mix. Resume normal fertilization with a fertilizer that contains chelated iron. Chelated iron is immediately available to plants. Quality hydroponic fertilizers contain chelated iron.

"I like 6-liter pails because 'Romulan' is a light feeder and it's easy to overfertilize. If a plant gets too much fertilizer, I can pick it up, put it in the sink and leach it easily.

Leaves with yellow patches are underfertilized. Nutrients are not available to the plant for one reason or another. Normally, nutrients are locked out with the wrong pH or there is a toxic fertilizer salt buildup in the growing medium. The solution to this condition is to leach pots with two gallons of water for every gallon of soil. Within a week of flushing the pots, normal growth will return and plants will be evenly green.

Overfertilization is evident when leaf tips are dark. Leaves curl under with the tip down in extreme cases of overfertilization. The solution for overfertilization: leach pots with two gallons of plain water for each gallon of soil. Wait until the next watering and leach pots again. Resume normal fertilization on the third watering. The affected leaves may not uncurl, but new growth will be strong and healthy with no new burned leaf tips.

'Romulan' Joe had an odor problem during the last two weeks before harvest. He found that the less he disturbed the plants during maintenance, the less they smelled. He lives in a windy area and smell is blown away immediately. To keep the smell out of the house 'Romulan' Joe uses a vent fan to evacuate stinky air up the chimney.

An odor puck helps keep air around the entrances to the house "fresh".

Harvest

(**Day 107**) "I've been growing 'Romulan' so long, I can bank on it being done in 56 days if I grow it right. The temperature, insects, disease and overfertilization are the things that make the crop take longer or produce less. I used to look at the glands with a jeweler's glass but I've grown it so long that I can tell when it's ready at a glance."

'Romulan' Joe cuts his plants off at the base and hangs the entire plant from a drying line strung across an open part of the vegetative room. He removes large leaves from the plants before hanging them to dry.

He puts Tanglefoot™ around drying lines to keep mites confined. As soon as the plants are cut, the sap dries up and mites start looking for live plants. Mites migrate from the harvested plant to live plants nearby. A barrier of Tanglefoot™ around the ends of drying lines will keep them from crossing. Except for jumpers, the Tanglefoot™ will subdue the balance.

Joe harvested 20 plants that rooted two weeks, vegetated five weeks, and flowered eight weeks. Dry bud weight averaged close to two ounces per plant, for a total of 36 ounces.

Harvesting and cleanup takes Joe a smoke-filled day.

Construction Supplies

Approximate Cost

Board, 1" x 12" x 3' shelf	$12
Board, 2 x 4s to frame room	$30
Board, 8-foot 2 x 4 for ceiling to hang lights from	$3
Cable ties to bundle wire	$5
Cloning Chamber	$60

    4 – 1" x 2" x 4'
    4 – 1" x 2" x 2'
    4 – 2" x 4" x 4'
    2 – 1/2" x 2' x 4' plywood

Sheet rock screws, hooks, chain, pulleys, ropes, fluorescent fixture for 2, 40-watt 4-foot tubes, plastic to cover chamber	$100
Deadbolt lock	$20
Door handle	$10
Drill, electric and drill bits	$0
Duct tape	$5
Ducting, flexible/expandable 8"	$30
Ducting, rigid 6"	$10
Fan, 800 CFM squirrel cage blower	$150
Fan, 240 CFM squirrel cage blower	$80
Fan, 3 – 16-inch circulation fans	$90
Flats – 2, 10" x 20" x 2" seedling flats with drainage	$5
Hardware (hooks, eyebolts, screws, chain, etc.)	$10
Hose, 50-feet 1/2-inch quality	$30
Jackhammer – one day rental	$70
Lights – two 600-watt HPS, one 400-watt HPS	$1000
Lights – dual fixture for 2, 40-watt fluorescent Tubes	$30
Plastic, Black/white Visqueen for walls	$50
Pump, 1250 GPH	$120
Pump-up quart spray bottle	$15
Reservoir, 33-gallon plastic garbage can	$15
Saw, electric circular	$30
Screwdriver, electric	$30
Sheet rock	$20
Solid-core pre-hung door	$100
Stapler	$5
Timer for lights	$30
Two pulleys and nylon cords to hang fluorescent fixture	$10
Thermostat/humidistat	$150
Utility knife	$5
Velcro for door	$10
Total	$2,340

Growing Supplies

Fertilizer – Nutrilife™	$20
Fungistat, Baking Soda	$5
Microscope, 30X	$50
Pesticide, Pyrethrum aerosol	$10
Pesticide, Pyrethrum concentrate to dilute in water	$10
Pesticide, Tanglefoot™	$10
Pots – 50, 4" pots, 50, 3-liter grow bags, 2, 20-gallon	$30
Pruners	$20
Rooting hormone jell	$10
Seeds: 'Romulan' – developed by grower	$0
Soilless mix – 8 cubic feet Sunshine #4, 1 cu. ft. SS #1	$30
Water can – 2-gallon	$20
Water wand with water/breaker/sprinkler head	$20
Total	**$2575**

Electricity

(also see chart in Appendix)
1200-watts (1.2) x 12 hrs x 30 days = 432 kilowatt-hours (KWH)
 400-watts (0.4) x 18 hrs x 30 days = 216 kilowatt-hours
   40 watts (0.04) x 24 hrs x 30 days = 29 kilowatt-hours
 432 + 216 + 29 = 677 kilowatt hours per month
677 x $0.10 (cost of KWH) = **$67.70** increase in monthly
electricity bill if electricity costs $0.10 per KWH.

$2465 setup cost
$67.70 - 30-day electricity bill
$67.70 - 30-day electricity bill
$ 2600.40 Total cost to grow first crop

$2600/36 ounces = **$72.20** per ounce for the first crop
$300/36 ounces = **$8.33** per ounce for each additional crop

Garden Calendar

This garden calendar is for three harvests. It begins assuming that there are two large mother plants.

Clone/root = 2 weeks (40 plants)
Veg. In 3-liter pails = 3 weeks (30 plants)
Veg. In 6-liter pails = 3 weeks
Flower in 6-liter pails = 8 weeks (20 plants)

1.	Take clones	January 1
2.	Transplant to 3-liter pails (18 hrs)	January 15
3.	Transplant to 6-liter pails (18 hrs)	February 5
4.	Induce flowering (12 hrs)	February 19
5.	Change to flowering fertilizer	February 19
6.	Stop fertilizing – feed plain water	March 19
7.	Harvest	April 16
8.	Take clones	March 12
9.	Transplant to 3-liter pails (18 hrs)	March 26
10.	Transplant to 6-liter pails (18 hrs)	April 16
11.	Induce flowering with 12-hour nights	April 30
12.	Change to flowering fertilizer	April 30
13.	Stop fertilizing – feed plain water	May 28
14.	Harvest	June 11
15.	Take clones	April 23
16.	Transplant to 3-liter pails (18 hrs)	May 7
17.	Transplant to 6-liter pails (18 hrs)	May 28
18.	Induce flowering (12 hrs)	June 11
19.	Change to flowering fertilizer	June 11
20.	Stop fertilizing – feed plain water	July 23
21.	Harvest	August 6

Growing Statistics

Yield: 2 pounds every 8 weeks
Lbs/1000-w/30 days: 0.83
Grams/watt/30 days: 0.38

Clone room:	Root 30 clones 14 days
Part of vegetative	four 40-watt GroLux fluorescent
room	tubes 24 hours per day
	Sunshine #1
Vegetative room:——	Grow 30 plants for 3 weeks
5 x 10 feet	one 400-watt HPS

Flowering room: 10 x 10 feet	18 hours per day three-liter pails of Sunshine #4 Grow 20 plants for 8 weeks Two 600-watt HPS 12 hours per day three-liter pails of Sunshine #4
Harvest:	12, 2 – 3-foot tall plants Average weight 1 – 2 ounces each.

Monthly electricity cost (@ $0.10 per KWH): $67.70
First crop cost: $2,600 ($72.20 per ounce)
Next crop cost: $300 ($8.30 per ounce)

• **To downsize his garden by 50 percent,** Joe would use two 40-watt fluorescent tubes, one 150-watt HP and one 600-watt sodium lamp. He would also be able to make his rooms smaller. All of his other construction expenses would be the same. The smaller lights generate less heat and a smaller fan could be installed, but this would not allow for expanding the room later. Joe's work load and harvest would also decrease.

Yield: 1 pound every 8 weeks
Lbs/1000-w/30 days: 0.83
Grams/watt/30 days: 0.38

Clone room:	Root 16 clones 14 days two 40-watt GroLux fluorescent tubes 24 hours per day Sunshine #1
Vegetative room: 3 x 3 feet	Grow 16 plants for 3 weeks one 150-watt HPS 18 hours per day three-liter pails of Sunshine #4
Flowering room: 5 x 5 feet	Grow 12 plants for 8 weeks one 600-watt HPS 12 hours per day three-liter pails of Sunshine #4
Harvest:	12, 2 – 3-foot tall plants Average weight 1 – 2 ounces each.

Monthly electricity cost (@ $0.10 per KWH): $33.85
First crop cost: $2000 total ($125.00 per ounce)
Next crop cost: $100 ($6.25 per ounce)

Chapter Three

'BC Big Bud' Bob's Garden

Growing Statistics:

Yield:	*6 pounds every 3 weeks*
Cost:	*1st crop: $5747*
	($49.89 per ounce)
	2nd crop: $1000
	($7.81 per ounce)
Space:	*10 x 12 feet, 12 x 27 feet*
Watts:	*10,160*

'BC Big Bud' Bob's Garden

Bob is a professional landscaper during the day, and grows 'BC Big Bud' in his basement at night. After work, he marches down the basement stairs through a locked solid oak door into a Garden of 'BC Big Bud' Eden.

Bob likes growing in the basement. A basement with concrete walls is easy to keep cool and it is easy to have a close to constant climate year round. Basements are out of the way, easy to secure and convenient.

Bob shared his experience, "Some of the worst places to grow are in barns or garages not attached to homes. I used to grow in an old shed. Some local kids broke in and took my crop. So I moved to a house with a basement".

Setting Up the Grow Room - Step-by-Step

Step One: Bob searched many neighborhoods to find the perfect grow house. Finally he settled on a home that had electric appliances and was heated with natural gas. He checked with the electric company to learn the previous tenant's power consumption. It was between $300 - $400 per month, about the same as Bob planned to use. Bob rented a 4-bedroom house in a nice neighborhood with several large basement rooms, one of which measures 12 x 27 feet with a 7 1/2-foot ceiling. Next to that room was a 12 x 18-foot room with a deep laundry room sink. The rooms were bare with only a little rubbish on the floor. He swept the rooms out before mopping the floor and wiping down the walls with a 5 percent bleach solution.

Bob's house also has an automatic garage door. He installed a separate manual lock on the garage door so thieves could not use a universal electronic garage door opener and break into the house.

Step Two: Bob went shopping for grow room supplies at the local lumber/hardware store and a garden center. He purchased all the supplies listed at the end of this chapter.

Upon returning home, he opened the garage door, drove in and closed it automatically. Bob unloaded the supplies from his van in the privacy of the locked garage. To Bob's neighbors, his returning home with a van full of grow room supplies was just like any other time he returned home. He moved the supplies the short distance down the stairs into the basement in a few minutes. Bob laid out all of his supplies on the floor of the spare room and took a visual inventory.

Step Three: Bob framed a wall across the 12 x 18-foot room with 2 x 4s on 36-inch centers to form a 10 x 12-foot mother/clone/vegetative room. Bob found all the information he needed to frame the room and add a pre-hung door at the local lumber/hardware store. Bob made a rough sketch of his proposed rooms and walls and showed it to the clerk at the lumber/hardware store. The clerk helped Bob plan the project and sold him all the necessary supplies.

Step Four: Bob covered the walls of the flowering room with black/white Visqueen plastic. He used a staple gun to affix the black/white plastic to the walls. He used duct tape to secure a few loose corners. He overlapped black/white plastic over the door to help seal off the room and make it airtight. Now the entire 12 x 27 flowering room is white. Next he covered the walls of the vegetative room with black/white plastic.

Step Five: Bob cut a duct hole in the wall of the flowering room for the 960 CFM axial fan. He installed 4 feet of 8-inch flexible ducting through the hole. He screwed two eye bolts into joists in the ceiling and suspended the fan from a piece of nylon rope. He used duct tape to attach one end of the 8-inch duct to the exhaust end of the 960 CFM axial fan. The other end of the duct is vented into a crawl space between the basement and the main floor.

Bob installed an ozone generator in the crawl space to neutralize odor during flowering. The ozone generator was easy to install. First, he figured out the square footage of the room and set the generator to turn on for a few minutes every hour. He installed an oscillating fan to mix the air before it is evacuated by the 400 CFM axial fan at the other end of the crawl space.

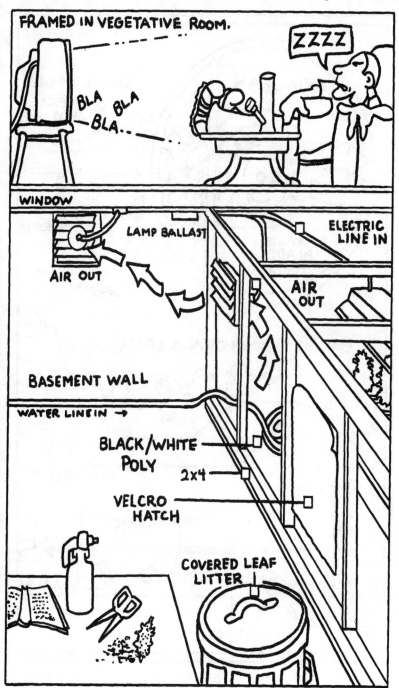

Bud and "J" framed in the vegetative room with 2 x 4s, installed lighting, water and ventilation.

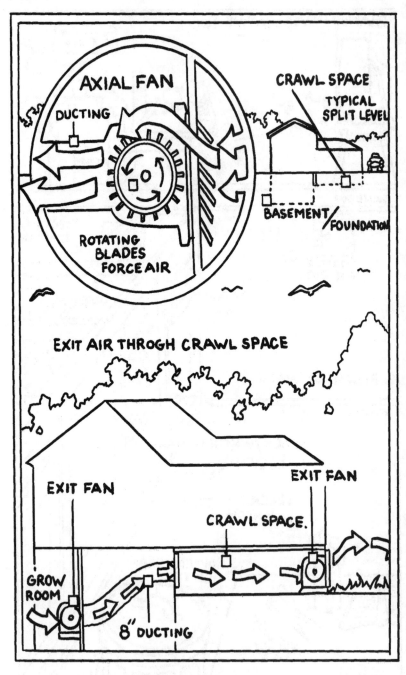

This cutaway drawing shows how a vent fan moves air from the grow room outdoors. Air is vented through ducting and the crawl space between floors, before it is vented outdoors.

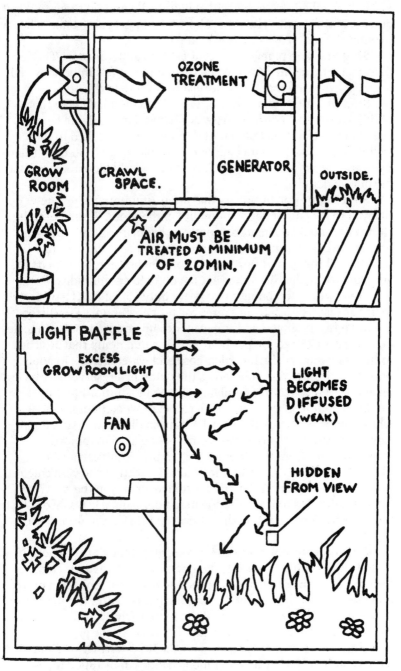

An ozone gererator located in the crawl space deodorizes air before it is moved outdoors. A light baffle diffuses grow room light and facilitates air movement.

Bob installed two vents with a light baffle around them to the outside of the room. The vents allow fresh, warm air from the house to enter the room. See drawing next page.

Step Six: Bob plugged the vent fan into a thermostat. The thermostat turns the fan on when the temperature climbs above 80 degrees. Now the room is white *and* well ventilated.

Step Seven: Bob attached 6, 16-inch oscillating fans to the ceiling with Bungi cords to increase air circulation. Table fans are less expensive and stay up out of the way when attached to the ceiling. The fans oscillate back and forth blowing air on the garden. They are not set in a fixed position, which would blow too hard and dry out tender plants.

Step Eight: Bob hung up a maximum/minimum hygrometer on the wall to measure relative humidity in the room. If the humidity climbs beyond 60 percent, Bob notices that plants grow slowly and have more health problems, but the exact cause is difficult to pinpoint. If the humidity climbs beyond 50 percent, Bob opens the door and manually turns the vent fan on to lower humidity.

Step Nine: Bob bought two heavy duty 55-gallon plastic barrels to use as reservoirs. He measures the proper amount of fertilizer into each reservoir and adds tap water to mix nutrient solution. He purchased a 1250 gallon per hour (GPH) sump pump that attaches to his lightweight °-inch garden hose and water wand. To apply nutrient solution, Bob submerges the pump in a reservoir, turns it on and starts fertigating (applying nutrient solution) plants.

Step Ten: In grow rooms with carpet or wood floors, a large white painter's dropcloth or thick visqueen plastic will save floors from moisture. A "wet/dry vacuum" can be used to remove standing water from the floor after watering. Trays can also be placed beneath each container for added protection and convenience. Bob's basement floor had a drain installed already in the concrete floor. He decided to leave the concrete floor bare. He washed it down with a 5 percent bleach solution and rinsed the floor with water.

Step Eleven: Bob screwed hooks strong enough to support 30 pounds into ceiling joists. He did not take any measurements, he just eyeballed the room and screwed the hooks in. Bob did a pretty good job of guessing where to hang the lights. After the lights were up and running, they illuminated the room fairly evenly. He used chain (adjustable) to hang the lamp fixtures over the garden.

The 12 x 27-foot room is lit with six 1000-watt HP sodium lamps and two 1000-watt super metal halide lamps (8000 total watts) with vertical parabolic dome reflectors. The bulbs (arc tubes) hang down below the bottom of the reflector and some of the unreflected light is wasted. Bulbs hang down between some plants and shine direct light on the garden, increasing efficiency somewhat. Changing to horizontal reflectors would increase useable light by 30 percent or more! With horizontal reflectors, there would be at least 30 percent more light, or nearly the equivalent of two more 1000-watt HP sodium lamps for the same amount of electricity used.

The 10 x 12-foot vegetative grow room is illuminated by two 1000-watt metal halide lamps hovering one foot above plants on a two-arm Sun Circle™. The Sun Circle™ is a device that moves the bulbs above the garden in a 360 degree circle. Bob likes the Sun Circle™ because it distributes bright light evenly over the garden. All the clones grow at the same rate and are the same size when moved into the flowering room. The vegetative room is where the clones establish a strong root system and grow into strong bushy babies. Bob's vegetative clones grow fast and seldom experience problems.

Bob runs the electrical cords along the ceiling, and back to the heat generating ballasts which he keeps outside the grow rooms to lower room temperature. He cut a hole in the wall and ran the ballast and cords through, then he built a shelf for the ballasts high on the wall outside of the grow room. The ballasts stay out of the way and are easy to inspect.

Step Twelve: Now Bob is ready to move 18-inch-tall rooted clones that have grown three weeks under 18 hours of light into the flowering room. Every three weeks, Bob moves 65 new 3-week-old clones (2 weeks of rooting and 3 weeks of vegetative growth) into the flowering room.

Crop Scheduling and Care

(Day 1) Clones are taken from four 'BC Big Bud' mother plants. Bob takes clones just like Lee in Chapter One. He puts a humidity tent on each tray of clones and moves them under the halides in the 18-hour room. He puts the clones 6 – 8 feet from the HID so that they receive less intense light.

The humidity tent over rooting clones helps them conserve moisture. The roots that will supply water to the clones are just starting to grow. High humidity during this tender stage in a clone's life keeps them from losing precious moisture. Bob opens the humidity tents two or three times a day to check on the rooting clones, and to mist them with plain water. Opening the humidity tent also allows fresh air circulation. Many times Bob leaves the humidity tent ajar so fresh air can circulate.

After two weeks of rooting, Bob transplants clones into 2-gallon pots and moves them into the 18-hour vegetative room. The 65 rooted clones stay under two 1000-watt metal halides mounted on a

The Sun Circle™ delivers more light for less money.

2-arm Sun Circle™ for three weeks. The clones grow into strong bushy plants by the time they are moved into the flowering room.

A total of 130 flowering clones are spaced about two-feet apart in two-gallon pots in the 324 square foot flowering room. Light shines on a room *full* of plants. Foliage *always* covers the entire floor. Pots are packed in just right so the plants barely touch one another and the walls. Bob achieves maximum harvests by keeping the room full at all times.

Two-gallon pots are definitely more work to water, but there are positive points to growing in two-gallon pots. The pots are easy to turn or move to a brighter location or elevate to a shelf. For example, Bob picks up two, two-gallon pots with each hand when he moves vegetative plants into the flowering room.

(Day 36) Bob moves the 65 bushy, 18-inch-tall clones into the 12-hour flowering room. He changes to a flowering fertilizer to promote bud growth.

Bob rotates his plants to keep his grow room full all the time. He harvests half the crop (65 plants) in the flowering room every three weeks. As harvest approaches, flowering females need brighter

Plants are everywhere in this flowering room. Light in the cloning chamber is obscured by plastic and does not effect flowering plants.

and brighter light to increase resin production. Plants to be harvested are placed directly under the brightest light during the last three weeks. Newly introduced plants are placed further away.

"I know the reflectors are not the best, so I had to compensate for that by setting the plants under the brightest light. I'm going to harvest the plants I set under the hottest (brightest) spots. They really flower out nice when they finish the last three weeks in the brightest light," assured Bob, as he lightly squeezed a ripe bud to release it's fragrance and took a whiff.

Bob places 65 new clones moved in for the next harvest on shelves around the perimeter of the garden. Elevating clones with shelves assures that they will receive more light. Shelves are simple to make. Bob sets two-gallon pots upside down under an 8-inch-wide plank/shelf with two-gallon clones set on top: an instant shelf.

The basement grow room stays close to the same temperature both winter and summer. Bob keeps the temperature of the house the same (65 degrees) all year round. The furnace heats the house in the winter. Bob keeps the flowering lights off and the house cool and closed during hot summer days. He turns the lights on and vents the house at night to keep it cool.

"I notice that when the temperature is a little warmer and cooler outside, it affects the temperature inside my grow room, even though it's in the basement. Yesterday was a few degrees cooler than the day before and the grow room was a little colder. I thought the lights and the fans would control the temperature perfectly, but the outside temperature affects the indoor temperature," Bob said looking a bit puzzled. "It's easier to control the grow room temperature when I keep the house at 65 degrees."

Bob feeds every third watering with General Hydroponics™ fertilizer and flushes all plants with plain water every four weeks, then adds fertilizer to the next watering. About 10 to 20 percent drains out onto the floor with each watering. The runoff carries away unwanted fertilizer salts. If leaves start to turn pale green or yellow, he fertilizes more often.

Bob mixes General Hydroponics™ fertilizer as per instructions and fertilizes plants when they are transplanted.

Bob also keeps the pH about 7 and he does not know the parts per million concentration of dissolved solids* in the nutrient solution. He seldom has problems with overfertilizing or under-fertilizing. He watches the health and growth rate of his plants to decide if they need more or less fertilizer.

· Footnote: The overall fertilizer strength in the nutrient solution can be measured in parts per million (PPM) of dissolved solids (DS) concentration. A small electronic PPM DS meter is inexpensive and easy-to-use. The Appendix contains a chart to

Upper Panel:
Wrap threads with Teflon tape to avoid dangerous leaks.
Lower Panel:
CO_2 can be generated by burning fossil fuel (propane,
butane, kerosene, etc.) or bottled in a tank and dispensed with a
metering system.

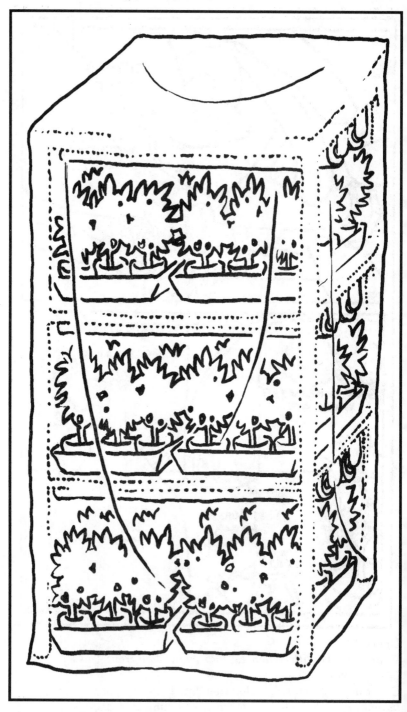

Clones root fast under a humidity tent.

convert from PPM to different nutrient solution measuring systems such as Electrical Conductivity (EC), and Conductivity Factor (CF).

Spider mites are Bob's biggest pest problem. He uses a homemade remedy that a friend gave him. "Einstein Oil" is now on the commercial market in Western Canada. It smells like rotten peanuts and has an organic neem oil base. (The neem tree, native to India, has been used as a natural insecticide for centuries. Today neem is the main ingredient in many other products, including disinfectant tooth paste and soap.) According to Bob: "I don't know what's in it, all I know is that it smells earthy and spicy and kills mites dead. He inspects plants daily for mites. Bob spot sprays any mite-damaged plants as soon as he sees them. He uses a pump-type sprayer with an application wand. The wand makes spraying under leaves, where spider mites live, easy and efficient.

CO_2 Enrichment

"When I added CO_2 to the flowering room, bud growth and weight increased by a half pound on every three-week crop," said Bob in a minor state of amazement.

Carbon dioxide (CO_2) naturally occurs in the air at the rate of 350 – 400 PPM (parts per million). However, plants can use up to 1500 PPM. When given more CO_2, plants grow faster, heavier and stronger. CO_2 is created by burning propane (or any fossil fuel) in an enclosed room. Grower's also use CO_2 injector systems that meter CO_2 into a room via a regulator, flow meter and timer.

Bob uses a CO_2 burner manufactured by Green Air Products, the CD 36. He keeps the CO_2 level between 1000 – 1500 PPM in the flowering room. The propane burned in the CO_2 unit adds a little heat and humidity to the room, a small inconvenience for the half-pound of buds added to each harvest. The pilot light ignites the CO_2 burner at timed intervals to bring the CO_2 level to 1500 PPM. CO_2 naturally occurs in the air at the rate of 350 – 400 PPM.

CO_2 is heavier than air and tends to stratify and sink. Six oscillating fans keep the heavier-than-air CO_2 well mixed with grow room air.

CO_2 generators also create heat and increase humidity. For each pound of gas burned, it will create about 22,000 BTU's (British Thermal Units) and 1-1/2 pounds of water. In small grow rooms, the heat and moisture produced by a CO_2 generator make it impractical to use. Growers with small rooms use bottled CO_2 that is emitted into the room at timed intervals.

Humans use low levels of CO_2. Levels above 0.4 percent (4000 PPM) could be hazardous to humans and plants if inhaled for long. The CO_2 level is easy to control with the proper metering system.

Misting plants several times a day with a hand sprayer adds humidity to the air and reduces stress.

Besides being hazardous to people and plants at high concentrations, plants cannot use CO_2 in levels above 0.15 percent (1500 PPM).

Wrap propane fitting threads with teflon tape before connecting to ensure a tight connection. To check your CO_2 system before using, apply a solution of 50 percent water and 50 percent concentrated dish soap to all connections, and check for leaks with pressure in the system. If bubbles appear, gas is escaping. Tighten fittings until bubbles no longer appear. Never use a leaky system!

Caution: Never overfill the propane tank! The gas will expand and contract with temperature change. Ask the attendant at the gas station about gas expansion when the outside temperature climbs.

To find out how much CO_2 it will take to bring the grow room up to the optimum level, Bob found the total volume of the grow room, then divided by the optimum level of CO_2.

Example:
Total Volume = Length x Width x Height
Total Volume = 12' x 27' x 8' = 2592 cubic feet
Total Volume = 2592 cubic feet
Optimum Level = .0015 (1500 PPM)
0.0015 x 2592 cubic feet = 3.8 cubic feet

It will take 3.8 cubic feet of CO_2 to bring the 2592 cubic foot grow room up to the optimum level.

Many growers prefer to locate the propane tanks outside of the grow room. Most city building codes require propane tanks outside of buildings in case they leak or explode.

Each 0.33 pound (5.3 ounces) of fossil fuel (kerosene, propane, natural gas, etc.) burned produces about one pound of CO_2. At 68 degrees, one lb. of CO_2 displaces 8.7 cubic feet of atmosphere.

$3.8 / 8.7 = \underline{0.44}$ x .33 = $\underline{0.145}$ pounds of fuel needed

$\underline{0.145}$ x 16 ounces = $\underline{2.32}$ ounces of fuel needed to bring the CO_2 level up to 1500 PPM.

To measure the amount of fuel used, weigh the tank before it is turned on, use it for one hour, then weigh it again. The difference in weight is the amount of fuel used.

It is easier and much less expensive to measure the amount of CO_2 produced rather than to measure the amount of CO_2 in the atmosphere of the grow room.

Bob knew it would be difficult to keep the temperature at 80 degrees and still get the most out of the CO_2 burner without spending a lot of money on monitoring devices and timers. He decided to turn the CO_2 burner on to bring the level of CO_2 up to 1500 PPM 3 – 4 times a day and let the vent fan exhaust the air as needed. He also installed the CO_2 generator in the opposite end of the room from the vent fan.

Harvest

(Day 78) Buds are so heavy the last two weeks before harvest that they must be staked. He takes extra care when watering and carefully moves sticky bud-laden branches out of his way. "Buds are packed with resin near harvest and tend to stick to anything that passes by. It's almost like they reach out and grab you," Bob said jumping away from a sticky bud.

"I'm growing 'Big Bud' or 'BC Big Bud', I'm not really sure which one it is, all I know is that it is one of the 'Big Bud' varieties. I like it because 'Big Bud' clones root easily, are easy to grow and produce a heavy harvest consistently", confirmed Bob.

Bob harvests 6 pounds every three weeks from 65 plants: a total of 12 pounds per 8 lights every 6 weeks from 130 plants. Bob is more concerned about volume than quality of bud because he sells his crop. He harvests plants about two weeks before peak ripeness so he can grow as many crops as possible in a year. If he grows only six, 8-week crops, he would harvest only 72 pounds a year. Growing 8 crops a year allows Bob to harvest two more crops, or a total of 96 pounds of dried buds every year.

Bob has a day job and it takes him a day or two to harvest and clean up the grow room before moving in 18-inch-tall clones and replanting the harvested half. He hauls away the used soil and hand-scrubs each pot in the laundry room sink with soap and water.

Bob spends one or two weekends a month manicuring harvested buds.

To harvest, Bob picks off large leaves before cutting plants off at the base with pruners. He hangs the entire plant on drying lines in the spare basement room. He harvests as fast as he can because this is when the smell of sweet success is the most pungent. Once the plants are stripped of large leaves and hanging in the drying room, Bob turns on two oscillating fans in the room to speed drying. He also sets an ozone generator in the room on a timer to remove odor. Bob set up a small 140 CFM vent van to move stinky air into the attic crawl space where it is treated with ozone and vented outdoors.

Bob has been growing for six years and had the most consistent results with soilless mix. He has grown in other hydroponic systems, but they were too complex for him. According to Bob: "Sunshine #4 (soilless mix) is forgiving and lets me make a few mistakes."

"I thought about changing to an automated hydroponic system, but I'm a little nervous about changing when my system works fine now. If I change, I think I would try the "Sea of Green", you know, grow lots of short plants on flood and drain tables in four-inch rockwool cubes. That would be the simplest system. I don't like to deal with all the complications. I'm a grower not a plumber!" Declared Bob.

Bob is a very good grower with a lot of experience, and he is very careful about changing systems, or even changing one thing in his grow room. His big experiment for the next crop is to pinch or prune the main stem. Bob plans to pinch the tops of a dozen plants so that they will grow more bushy. He will measure the dry bud weight of the pinched clones against the dry weight of a dozen unpinched plants to see which weighs more.

Much of Bob's success is due to his attention to detail, quick response time to problems and his perseverance. Bob fixes all problems immediately. He does not wait to clean up, cleanup is perpetual. If he sees any type of problem: spider mite, water on the floor, dry pot, dirty bulb, etc., he fixes it at once. He never lets anything slide. He makes sure to grow in a clean, healthy environment all the time. For example, Bob starts watering and does not stop until he is finished. This way he is able to keep track of which plants have been watered and which have not.

Chart on cubic feet of room and how much CO_2
it takes to bring level up to 1500 PPM

To find out how much CO_2 it will take to bring a grow room up to the optimum level, Bob followed the example below and inserted the appropriate figures in the blanks.

Example:
Total Volume = Length x Width x Height = total cubic feet
Total Volume = _____' x _____' x _____' = _____ total
cubic feet

Total cubic feet x 1500 PPM = cubic feet CO_2
needed to bring level to 1500 PPM

_____ x 0.0015 = _____ cubic feet

_____/8.7 = _____ x 0.33 = _____ pounds
of fuel needed

_____ x 16 = _____ ounces of fuel needed to bring
the CO_2 level up to 1500 PPM.

"I'm getting tired of spending over an hour watering almost every day. If I automated the irrigation, my day would be easier," sighed Bob.

I looked at Bob and said: "I'll show you how to make your day easier . . . smoke this."

Construction Supplies
Approximate Cost

Bleach	$5
Boards, 2" x 4" to frame 12 feet of wall	$50
Boards, 1 x 8-inches for plant shelving	$50
Board 1 x 12-inch for shelf for ballasts	$5
Brackets for ballast shelf	$5
Bungi cords	$15
CO_2 generator with 5-gallon propane tank	$300
Door, pre-hung for vegetative room	$50
Ducting, 8-inch, 10-feet flexible	$15
Fan, 960 CFM axial vent fan for flowering room –	$200
Fans, 8, 16-inch oscillating circulation fans	$300
Fan, 400 CFM axial vent fan for attic	$140
Fan, 140 CFM vent for drying room	$80
Flats, 6 with humidity tents	$10
Hardware (hooks, screws, chain, etc.)	$10
Hygrometer	$10
Lights – 6, 100-watt HPS, 4, 1000-watt MH	$2400
Lock, for garage door	$5
Lock – deadbolt –	$20
Ozone generator	$300
Pump, 1250 GPH –	$120
Reservoir, 55-gallon plastic barrel	$30
Screws, sheet rock	$5
Sheet metal for heat guard	$10
Staple gun and staples	$25
Sun Circle™, 2-arm	$250
Tape, duct tape –	$5
Tape, Teflon for CO_2 generator connections	$5
Thermostat –	$40
Timer for lights	$100
Vents, 2 for fresh air	$10
Visqueen plastic –black/white	$40
White paint, 3-inch paint brush, roller and paint pan	$30

Total   **$4,640**

SEX

Background:
Pollen sacks on this
blooming male are
beginning to open
and shed pollen.

ale plants show their sex a
w weeks before flowering.
Look for a single spur at
branch unions.

Females show their sex
about the same time as male
plants. A pair of early white
pistils at branch unions
means she's a girl.

CLONING

Cut a branch to make a clone.

Trim leaves and excess
foliage from the clone.

Dip the clone
in rooting jell.

Insert the clone in a pre-
made hole in a flat full of
soilless mix.

Root clones under a humidity tent
and fluorescent light.

Rooted clone in
soilless
mix two weeks
later.

Background:
Close-up of spider mites swarming on the tip of a dead male plant. Mites enveloped this infested flower in spider webs. At death, mites ascend the pinnacle searching for a living home.

Plant
PROBLEMS

Leaf with heavy spider mite damage is evidenced by stippling marks. The leaf also shows signs of nutrient deficiency.

Nitrogen deficient leaf.

Burned tips, curled down, or shiny, brittle leaves are different signs of over fertilization. This bud has them all!

Whitish stippling marks left by spider mites cripple growth. Discolored leaf edges show fertilizer toxicity.

Tammy Faye's Bedroom Garden

...lexible yellow drain hoses ...arry nutrient solution back to the reservoir in Tammy Faye's Garden.

Barge (background) inspecting huge 'Champaign' buds.

A Canadian "twonie" lends perspetive to this huge six-month-old female trunk.

...is root mass grew during ...ight weeks of flowering.

...kground: Joe's garden packed with 'Romulan'

'Champagne' bud in full bloom, about ten days before harvest.

'BC BIG BUD

Above: Clones grow strong roots with high humidity and flourescent light.

Upper Right: Transplanted clones bush out under three weeks of metal halide light, with tall mothers in the background.

Background: The same crop three weeks later.

Right: Bushy 'BC Big Bud' is ready to go into the flowering room.

Above: Bud uses a watering wand to irrigate pots in between dense foliage.

Right: Hanging the bulbs in between the plants compensates for inefficient reflectors.

BOB'S GARDEN

Close-up of 'BC Big Bud' after six weeks of flowering.

Below: "BC Big Bud" on harvest day.

ve:
1000-watt HP-sodiums and two 1000-watt halides
ply light to a room full of 'BC Big Bud.'
of the crop is two weeks from harvest.

Right: On harvest day. Obese buds have been staked, and an extra entilation fan was added to lower the humidity, preventing bud mold.

#1

#2

#3

#4

#5

Bud &'J LOVE Frost

#1 - Clones in Oasis™ cubes grow roots in 14 days under flourescent lights.
#2 - Strong roots ensure this clone, a week into flowering, will produce a bountiful harvest.
#3 - Lower leaves receive little light and are removed the first week of flowering. Spaghetti irrigation tubes are also easier to see and maintain.
#4 - Leaves yellow soon after fertilizer is witheld, which flushes the chemical taste from the buds.

#6

#7

#8

#9

#5 - Overall view of Bud and 'J's' tube garden. The 40-gallon reservoir in the middle is replenished every day during peak growth.

#6 - Sticky "finger hash" is scraped off hands to make high quality smoke.

#7 - Huge buds with the large leaves removed, ready for harvest.

#8 - Close-up of 'Champagne' in full bloom.

#9 - Bud Love and 'J' Frost's "Avenue of the Giants"

Background Both Pages - Extreme close-up of 'Champagne' in full bloom.

'Blueberry' in full bloom.

Close up of a 'Northern Lights' x 'Blueberry' cross.

5 Easy Buds

'White Widow' is one of the most potent indoor varieties available.

Breeder Steve's thumb parts seed bracts on a bud of 'Shiskeberry.'

Background:
Fresh 'BC Big Bud' will dry in this rack in about five days.

Grow Supplies

Fertilizer – General Hydroponics™	$20
Hose, 1/2-inch x 50 feet	$30
Pesticide, Einstein Oil	$10
Pots, 150, 2-gallon –	$80
Pruners –	$20
Rooting jell –	$10
Soilless mix, 4 cubic foot bags Sunshine #4	$100
Sprayer, 1.5 gallon pump up	$20
Water can, 2-gallon	$10
Water wand with water breaker –	$15

Total   **$4955.00**

Electricity: (also see chart in Appendix)
8000-watts (8) x 12 hrs x 30 days = 2880 kilowatt-hours (KWH)
2000-watts (2) x 18 hrs x 30 days = 1080 KWH
2880 + 1080 = 3960 kilowatt hours per month
3960 x $0.10 (cost of KWH) = $396.00 increase in monthly
electricity bill if electricity costs $0.10 per KWH.

$4955.00 setup cost
$396.00 - 30-day electricity bill
$396.00 - 30-day electricity bill
$5747.00 Total cost to grow first crop

$5747/128 ounces = **$44.89** per ounce for the first crop
$1000/128 ounces = **$7.81** per ounce for each additional crop

Garden Calendar

This garden calendar is for four harvests. It begins assuming
that there are four large mother plants.

1.	Take clones	January 1
2.	Transplant to 2-gallon pots (18 hrs)	January 15
3.	Induce flowering (12 hrs)	February 5
4.	Change to flowering fertilizer	February 5
5.	Harvest	March 19
6.	Take clones	January 22
7.	Transplant to 2-gallon pots (18 hrs)	February 5
8.	Induce flowering (12 hrs)	February 26
9.	Change to flowering fertilizer	February 26

10.	Harvest	April 9
11.	Take clones	Feb. 12
12.	Transplant to 2-gallon pots (18 hrs)	Feb. 26
13.	Induce flowering (12 hrs)	March 19
14.	Change to flowering fertilizer	March 19
15.	Harvest	April 30
16.	Take clones	March 5
17.	Transplant to 2-gallon pots (18 hrs)	March 19
18.	Induce flowering (12 hrs)	April 9
19.	Change to flowering fertilizer	April 9
20.	Harvest	May 21

Growing Statistics

Yield: 6 pounds every 3 weeks
(6-week rotating harvest)

Lbs/1000-w/30 days: 1
Grams/watt/30 days: 0.45

Clone room: Root 70 clones 14 days
Part of vegetative four, 40-watt GroLux fluorescent
room tubes 24 hours per day
Sunshine #1

Vegetative room: Grow 70 plants for 3 weeks
10 x 12 feet two 1000-watt metal halides on 2-
arm Sun Circle™
18 hours per day
two-gallon pots of Sunshine #4

Flowering room: Grow 130 plants for 6 weeks
12 x 27 feet six 1000-watt HPS, two 1000-watt
metal halides
12 hours per day
three-gallon pots of Sunshine #4

Harvest: 65, 2 – 3-foot tall plants
Average weight 1– 1-1/2 ounces
each.

Monthly electricity cost (@ $0.10 per KWH): $396
First crop cost: $5747 total (**$49.89** per ounce)
Next crop cost: $1000 (**$7.81** per ounce)

To downsize his garden by 50 percent, Bob would use two 40-watt fluorescent tubes, one 1000-watt HP sodium and four 1000-watt HP sodium lamps. He would also be able to make his rooms half the original size. Most of the other construction expenses would be the same. The smaller lights generate less heat and a smaller fan could be installed. Bob's work load and harvest would also decrease.

Yield:	3 pounds every 3 weeks
	(6-week rotating harvest)
Lbs/1000-w/30 days:	1
Grams/watt/30 days:	0.45
Clone room:	Root 35 clones 14 days
Part of vegetative	two, 40-watt GroLux fluorescent
room	tubes 24 hours per day
	Sunshine #1
Vegetative room:	Grow 35 plants for 3 weeks
8 x 10 feet	1000-watt metal halide
	18 hours per day
	two-gallon pots of Sunshine #4
Flowering room:	Grow 66 plants for 6 weeks
10 x 16 feet	four 1000-watt HPS
	12 hours per day
	three-gallon pots of Sunshine #4
Harvest:	66, 2 – 3-foot tall plants
	Average weight 1 – 1 ° ounces each.

Monthly electricity cost (@ $0.10 per KWH): $198
First crop cost: $3534 total (**$73.62** per ounce)
Next crop cost: $500 (**$10.41** per ounce)

To downsize his garden by 85 percent, Bob would use one 400-watt HP sodium and two 600-watt HP sodium lamps. He would also be able to make his rooms proportionately smaller. The room could be so small that a CO_2 generator would generate too much heat. He could substitute a CO_2 injector system for the CO_2 generator. Much of his other construction expenses would be the same. The smaller lights generate less heat and a smaller fan could be installed. Bob's work load and harvest would also decrease.

Yield:	14 ounces every 3 weeks
	(6-week rotating harvest)
Lbs/1000-w/30 days:	1
Grams/watt/30 days:	0.45
Clone room:	Root 12 clones 14 days
Part of vegetative room	18 hours per day
	Sunshine #1
Vegetative room:	Grow 12 plants for 3 weeks
5 x 5 feet	one 400-watt HP sodium
	18 hours per day
	two-gallon pots of Sunshine #4
Flowering room:	Grow 10 plants for 6 weeks
10 x 10 feet	two 600-watt HPS
	12 hours per day
	three-gallon pots of Sunshine #4
Harvest:	10, 2 – 3-foot tall plants
	Average weight 1 – 1 ° ounces each.

Monthly electricity cost (@ $0.10 per KWH): $60
First crop cost: $2680 total ($191.42 per ounce)
Next crop cost: $150 ($10.71 per ounce)

Chapter Four
Tammy Fay's Bedroom Garden

Growing Statistics

Yield:	*2 pounds every 8 weeks*
Cost:	*1ˢᵗ crop $3312 ($103.50 per ounce)*
	2ⁿᵈ crop: $300 ($9.38 per ounce)
Space:	*10 x 12 feet, 12 x 27 feet*
Watts:	*2480*

Tammy Fay's Bedroom Garden

Tammy Fay knows how to nurture plants, and they respond. A natural grower, Tammy Fay cultivates a few large plants in the safe, friendly environment of her home. Soil is her favorite growing medium, but disposal presents a problem. She chose the next best thing to an organic soil garden, a hydroponic garden with organic fertilizer.

Tammy Fay grows eight large plants in a top feed hydroponic bucket system. The hydroponic garden consists of a reservoir, 8, five-gallon buckets, each with one-gallon net pots filled with "Hydroclay" and watered/fertilized (fertigated) via spaghetti tubes. The nutrient solution flows over the Hydroclay and roots down into the five-gallon container and out of the drain back to the reservoir.

Growing a great crop in a top feed hydroponic bucket system is simple and easy. Tammy Fay chose this system not only because it is simple and easy; growing only 8 large plants keeps Tammy Fay's total number of plants below thirty: 8 flowering plants, 2 – 3 mother plants and 15 – 20 clones for the next crop.

"The harvest from my babies pays our bills. I send my daughter to private school and this crop makes everything work out," explained Tammy Fay.

Setting Up the Grow Room: Step-by-Step

Step One: A spare bedroom at one end of Tammy Fay's home serves as the flowering room. The mother/vegetative/cloning rooms are located in the large closet in the same bedroom.

The bedroom measures 12 x 14 feet with an 8-foot ceiling. The closet is 3-1/2 feet deep, 8 feet wide and 8 feet high with large door that fold open across the 8-foot front. The bedroom and closet were already painted an off white, so Tammy Fay decided to grow in the rooms without painting them. She did cover the carpeted floor with heavy-duty Visqueen plastic to protect it from moisture.

Mini-blinds and curtains cover the bedroom window. Tammy Fay used duct tape to fasten a large, double-thick, piece of black/ white Visqueen plastic over the curtains. No light can be seen from outside the bedroom.

Step Two: She bought her hydroponic system at one of the many hydroponic stores located in North America. There are many similar bucket systems that the nutrient solution drains back to the reservoir effectively.

To install the hydroponic system, Tammy Fay followed the manufacturer's assembly instructions. She took inventory to ensure all the pieces were included before she assembled the system.

She set up four buckets around each lamp. The lamp will hang down in between the plants, lighting foliage on the top and sides.

"I decided to buy the hydroponic systems instead of trying to make my own. I know this system works. I saw it work at the store where I bought it. I'm a good grower, I like plants and I like to garden. I don't have time to reinvent my own hydroponic system. I spend my time on things I like to do," said Tammy Fay with a self-assured smile.

A flexible 3/4-inch drain hose is attached to each bucket. The flexible hose allows the buckets about a foot of movement in each direction. The buckets are moved closer to the light when they contain a small plant and farther away as the plant grows larger.

She assembled the spaghetti tube irrigation system and ran each tube to one of the 5-gallon containers. Soon the reservoir was set up and the system was ready for a pressure test.

Once the system was completely assembled, she filled the reservoir with water and started the pump. This step is very important. Tammy Fay checked all the hose connections for leaks. She also checked all the lines to make sure water flowed through properly.

She tightened two drain hoses that had small leaks and cleared a small piece of plastic lodged in one of the spaghetti tubes.

Step Three: Tammy Fay used large hooks to hang two 1000-watt HP sodium lamps vertically, with no reflective hoods. The bulbs hang down between the large plants. Plants receive only direct light from the bulb.

Foliage receives uneven light and plants need to be turned every few days. Turning plants is very easy with this bucket system.

Tammy Fay turns the one-gallon net pot containing the plant. She turns them one way in quarter turns, then back the other way in quarter turns so roots do not become tangled.

Step Four: Tammy Fay cut a hole in the ceiling for the hot stale grow room air to vent out. She predrilled holes in the ceiling joists to attach the 400-CFM vent fan to the ceiling. She sandwiched thick felt grommets between the ceiling and the vent fan to deaden noisy vibrations before securing it with lag bolts to ceiling joists.

The exhaust fan vented up through the ceiling in the one-level home. Once in the attic, the air blew out through the vents in the attic. Sometimes the sweet smell of flowering marijuana becomes overwhelming and she turns on the ozone generator in the attic. Tammy Fay is careful to keep the ozone generator "on" time to a minimum. The tale-tale smell of ozone can be as difficult to explain as the sweet bouquet of flowering marijuana.

Tammy Fay set up two 16-inch oscillating fans at each corner of the flowering room to circulate the air both day and night.

Step Five: The front doors of the closet vegetative/mother room have see-through louvers. Tammy Fay used duct tape to fasten black/white plastic over the louvers on the doors to block out light. She also cut a large piece of plastic to drape completely over the doors to block out all light. She rolls the plastic up and ties it up above the doors when she needs access to the mother/vegetative room. To increase air circulation, she opens the door to the mother/clone room when the light is on in the adjacent flowering room.

Tammy Fay hung a 400-watt HP sodium lamp from a hook in the ceiling inside the closet. She placed the remote ballast outside on the flowering room floor. She oriented the bulb parallel to the 3 °-foot wall so the footprint of the light would be most effective.

Tammy Fay set up a 12-inch oscillating fan to circulate air in the room. The circulation fan also acted as a vent fan. It blows air out some of the cracks in the doors of the small room.

She bought a 3-foot-square flood and drain hydroponic system that included: a table, reservoir, timer, pump and connecting plumbing to irrigate the table automatically with spaghetti tubes. She set it up according to the manufacturer's instructions. Tammy Fay filled the reservoir and turned the pump on. She checked for leaks and found none.

Step Six: To make the cloning chamber in the closet grow room, Tammy Fay installed a 3 x 4-foot shelf 3 feet high at one end of the closet. Tammy Fay used "L" brackets with screws to install the shelf/top of the cloning chamber. Below the shelf/top she hung a 4-foot fluorescent fixture containing two, 40-watt fluorescent tubes (one Cool White and one Warm White) to form a cloning chamber. She draped black/white plastic over the front and sides of the shelf/

top to make a door. She controls the humidity of the cloning room by misting clones with water several times a day. As the water evaporates into the air, humidity climbs. To lower humidity and increase air circulation, Tammy Fay opens the plastic cloning chamber door once or twice daily.

Garden Care

Tammy Fay changes the nutrient solution every 4 – 7 days when she harvests a plant.

She uses the reservoir pump to pump nutrient solution out into the outdoor garden.

The 5-gallon bucket garden stays irrigated 24 hours a day. The nutrient solution flows from the 1/8-inch spaghetti tubing all the time so the pump needs no timer. The secret to this system is to keep the water flowing over the roots. When water is stagnant, or roots become dry is when problems occur. Strong healthy roots and plants have the ability to outgrow minor fungus or insect attacks.

Tammy Fay must keep an ever-vigilant eye out for fungus and spider mites. Since she is growing large plants, harvesting and planting one plant every 4 – 7 days, plants are never totally removed so the room can be cleaned. Once insects or fungus get started, they can be very difficult to remove.

Tammy Fay spot sprays with aerosol pyrethrum whenever she sees signs of spider mites.

The vent fan keeps the temperature at 75 degrees F. She also turns the flowering light on from 7 PM – 7 AM to keep the room cool. Keeping the reservoir covered helps minimize humidity buildup.

Each of eight, five-gallon buckets have a one-gallon net pot filled with Hydroclay set in a round hole cut in the top of the bucket. Each bucket is watered with a 1/8-inch spaghetti tube. The irrigation tube is kept 1 – 2 inches away from the trunk of the plant. Too much water on the trunk causes it to rot. Once applied, the nutrient solution drains through the Hydroclay, down the cascading roots, and out the drain to the reservoir. A submersible 320-gallon per hour (GPH) pump in the reservoir keeps the nutrient solution moving. The roots are in a perfect environment to grow well. By the end of the crop, roots have formed a huge mat on the bottom of the bucket.

The last three weeks of flowering, Tammy Fay bends the branches, instead of turning plants to receive more light. She uses garden wire to train the branches into positions where they will receive the most light and not shade other plants.

Tammy Fay grows exclusively with organic Earth Juice™ because she loves the taste of organically grown marijuana. She is not able to flush the fertilizer taste from individual plants because she grows in a system with a connected irrigation system and a perpetual harvest. Natural organic Earth Juice™ fertilizer leaves the dried buds with a pleasant earthy taste, rather than a raspy chemical taste. Tammy Fay tops the reservoir off with plain water between emptying and refilling the reservoir with fresh nutrient solution.

Few yellow leaves appear on plants. The only yellow leaves appear near the bottom of the plants where they receive little light.

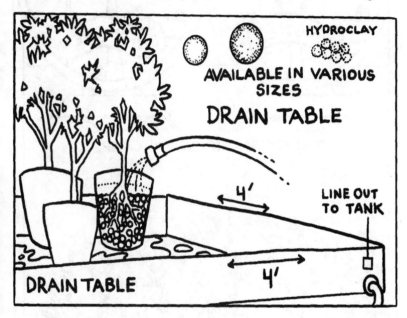

The flood and drain table in the vegetative closet room makes watering quick and easy. Flushing hydroclay from the top washes away salt buildup.

Clones

(Day 1) She takes 2 – 4 cuttings a week from larger female plants and roots them in rockwool cubes. See Chapter Five for more information on cloning. She places the cuttings under the dual bulb 80-watt fluorescent stoplight in the cloning room. She keeps 10 to 15 clones rooting at all times. About half of the clones are moved to the flowering room. She dries and smokes the others.

NOTE: Taking clones from mothers that have received only 18 hours or more of daily light is the key to maintaining genetic integrity in clones. Every time a clone is taken from a mother plant

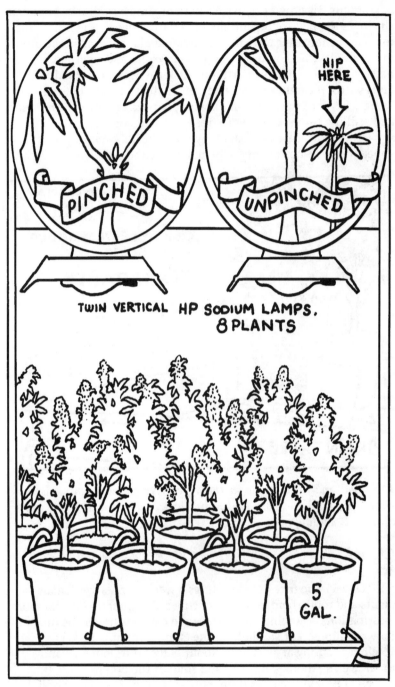

Tammy Faye pinches some plants to make them bushier and retard flowering.

Black/white plastic blocks light from the vegetative closet grow room. Tammy Faye rolls up the plastic to open the closet doors.

that has flowered and reverted back to vegetative growth, the clone will lose potency or other dominant characteristics. For example, if you have an original page of text and you photocopy this page and make a photocopy of that photocopy, the last copy is not as crisp and clean as the original. This example is similar with clones taken from rejuvenated female marijuana plants.

(Day 21) Once the clones are rooted, they are transplanted into one-gallon net pots filled with Hydroclay and placed on a flood and drain table under a 400-watt HP sodium lamp in the closet vegetative room. Tammy Fay pours nutrient solution over the plants several times a day for the first three or four days to ensure strong root growth into the Hydroclay. If a profuse root system does not grow down into the clay pellets before being moved into the big pots, growth slows substantially. Tammy Fay inspects roots regularly to ensure adequate nutrient solution flow over the roots. She inspects roots during both vegetative growth and flowering growth.

A small 120 GPH pump moves nutrient solution from a 20-gallon reservoir under the table through a 1/2-inch manifold attached to 1/8-inch spaghetti tubes to the plants. There are 15, 1/8-inch spaghetti tubes attached to the manifold. She puts as many feeder tubes around the plants as necessary to ensure a good flow of nutrient solution through the one-gallon net pot full of Hydroclay.

Clones stay under 18 hours of vegetative light three or four weeks or until they are two feet tall, strong and bushy. For every two clones that make it to this stage, Tammy Fay moves only one into the flowering room.

(Day 42) Tammy Fay moves one 2-foot-tall clone into the empty 5-gallon pot in the flowering room every 4 – 7 days.

Harvest

(Day 102) Tammy Fay harvests one plant every 4 or 5 days. She harvests her varieties after 8 – 8-1/2 weeks of flowering, that's when the resin crystals are ready to burst.

Each plant weighs about 3 – 4 ounces, depending on variety. When she harvests a plant, she flushes the entire system with plain water and scrubs out the bucket of the harvested plant. Next she refills the reservoir and adds Earth Juice™ flowering formula as per instructions.

To harvest, Tammy Fay removes the wire ties holding bent branches, and harvests large bud-laden branches individually. She cuts branches with pruners and picks off large leaves before manicuring fresh buds. After manicuring, Tammy Fay hangs the large branches in a large cardboard box from drying lines. The box absorbs much of the moisture from the foliage. To vent the box, Tammy Fay simply opens the top.

Tammy Fay cleans the Hydroclay by dumping the contents of a net pot in a 5-gallon bucket of water. She pulls most of the roots out by hand. Many of the roots float to the top of the water, other roots sink to the bottom. She tosses the Hydroclay in a large colander and rinses the Hydroclay before it is ready for the next crop.

The Happy Harvester

Construction Supplies
Approximate Cost

Drill, electric and drill bits –	$0
Fan, 400 CFM vent	$150
Fan, 2 – 16-inch circulation fans	$50
Fan, 12-inch oscillating circulation	$20
Felt for fan grommets	$10
Hardware (hooks, screws, chain, etc.)	$10
Hydroponic system, 8-bucket	$800
Hydroponic system, flood & drain	$400
Lights – two 1000-watt	$700
Lights - one 400-watt HPS	$250
Lights, two 40-watt fluorescent bulbs and fixture	$30
Ozone generator	$300
Plastic, black/white Visqueen for walls	$50
Saw, hand	$10
Screwdriver, electric	$30
Timer for lights	$30
Thermostat/humidistat	$150

Grow Supplies

Fertilizer – Earth Juice™	$20
Flats – 2, 10" x 20" x 2" seedling flats with drainage	$5
pH meter	$30
Pesticide, Pyrethrum aerosol	$10
Pruners	$20
Pump-up quart spray bottle	$15
Rooting hormone jell	$10
Water can – 2-gallon	$20
Wire ties to keep bent branches in place	$5

Total $3125

Electricity

(also see chart in Appendix)
2000-watts (2) x 12 hrs x 30 days = 720 kilowatt-hours (KWH)
400-watts (0.4) x 18 hrs x 30 days = 216 kilowatt-hours
720 + 216 = 936 kilowatt hours per month
936 x $0.10 (cost of KWH) = $93.60 increase in monthly
electricity bill if electricity costs $0.10 per KWH.

$3125 setup cost
$93.60 - 30-day electricity bill
$93.60 - 30-day electricity bill
$3312.20 Total cost to grow first crop

$3312/32 ounces = $103.50 per ounce for the first crop
$300/32 ounces = $9.38 per ounce for each additional crop

Garden Calendar

Take 2 – 4 clones – every 4 – 7 days.
Transplant clones to one-gallon net pots on flood & drain table
– every 4 – 7 days.
Harvest one plant in 5-gallon hydroponic system – every 4 – 7 days.
Move clone in net pot into flowering room – every 4 – 7 days.

Growing Statistics

Yield:	2 pounds every 8 weeks
Lbs/1000-w/30 days:	1
Grams/watt/30 days:	0.45
Clone room:	Root 15 – 20 clones 21 days
Part of vegetative	two, 40-watt fluorescent tubes
room	18 hours per day
	Rockwool cubes
Vegetative room:	Grow 10 – 15 plants for 3 – 4 weeks
10 x 12 feet	one 400-watt HP sodium
	18 hours per day
	one-gallon net pots of Hydroclay
Flowering room:	Grow 8 plants for 8 weeks
12 x 27 feet	two 1000-watt HPS
	12 hours per day
	top-feed hydroponic bucket system
Harvest:	8, 3 – 5-foot tall plants
	Weight 3 – 4 ounces each.

Monthly electricity cost (@ $0.10 per KWH): $93.60
First crop cost: $3,312 total (**$103.50** per ounce)
Next crop cost: $300 (**$9.38** per ounce)

• **To downsize her garden by 50 percent,** Tammy Fay would use two 40-watt fluorescent tubes one 1000-watt HP sodium lamp. She could also decrease the size of the rooms by half. Most of the other construction expenses would be the same. Less wattage generates less heat, and a smaller fan could be installed. Tammy Fay would have to work less and her harvest would also decrease.

Yield:	1 pound every 8 weeks
	(2 ounces per week)
Lbs/1000-w/30 days:	1
Grams/watt/30 days:	0.45
Clone room:	Root 8 – 10 clones 21days
Part of vegetative	two 150-watt HP sodiums
room	18 hours per day
	Rockwool cubes
Vegetative room:	Grow 5 – 8 plants for 3 – 4 weeks
10 x 12 feet	two 150-watt HP sodium2
	18 hours per day
	one-gallon net pots of Hydroclay
Flowering room:	Grow 4 plants for 8 weeks
12 x 27 feet	one 1000-watt HPS
	12 hours per day
	top-feed hydroponic bucket system
Harvest:	4, 3 – 5-foot tall plants
	Weight 3 – 4 ounces each.

Monthly electricity cost *(@ $0.10 per KWH)*: $46.80
First crop cost: $1750 total (**$109.38** per ounce)
Next crop cost: $150 (**$9.38** per ounce)

Chapter Five

Bud Love & "J" Frost's Hydro Tube Garden

Growing Statistics

Yield:	*6 pounds every 3 weeks*
Cost:	*1ˢᵗ crop: $5880 ($61.25 per ounce)*
	2ⁿᵈ crop: $700 ($7.25 per ounce)
Space:	*10 x 10 feet, 10 x 10 feet*
Watts:	*6960*

Bud Love & "J" Frost's Hydro Tube Garden

Bud Love and "J" Frost pooled their resources six months ago to rent a house and grow a garden to escape their day jobs. Their lucrative hobby soon turned into full time employment.

Security was their number one concern since they are growing more than 99 plants and living in America, land of the free. They soon found their personal lives radically changed while they fill the ever-increasing demand for quality marijuana.

Choosing a grow house was their most important security decision. They spent more than a month visiting rental houses every day before they found the perfect house. The previous residents used a lot of electricity. They asked the landlord and checked with the electric company for the past tenant's electrical consumption. That's right, the electric company gave them information that they were unauthorized to give. The house also had an electric furnace, an electric hot water heater, electric oven and dishwasher. After they moved in, the grow lights used nearly the same amount of electricity as the previous tenants.

The growers decided that the landlord's personality is as important as choosing which variety to grow. Once they found several suitable houses, they carefully interviewed each owner/landlord to learn their habits including how much time they have to come over and annoy them. They finally settled on the ideal landlord, a very busy person that preferred minimum contact with them. The landlord lives out of town, has a full life , young children and a demanding job, all signs that the tenants would be left alone. Before signing the contract, the landlord agreed the house was up to code, which ensured no unnecessary visits by local inspectors, appraisers or repairmen.

Retired landlords, especially if they used to live at the house they want to rent to you, come back to work on the garden, house or whatever, just like they still live there. They also have time to come and work on the house. According to "J": "The landlord can live in the same town or out of town, the main quality to look for is that they do not have a meddlesome personality."

The house was rented by a foreign relative visiting from Holland. The relative also opened an account at the electric and telephone companies before she returned to Holland. Bills come to the house and are paid with a cashier's check within 48 hours. If a problem occurs at the house, Bud and "J" have the option of walking away and never looking back.

Their house has plenty of privacy. From the outside, no neighbors can see the entire inside of the house. The house has an open look and is still within a private setting. An automatic, double garage door lets them load and unload the car in complete privacy. They put a separate manual lock on the automatic garage door so thieves could not use a master opener to break in.

The outside of the house and the garden are well-kept and look like the other houses in the neighborhood. They changed the locks to the grow rooms. The exterior door lock remains the same. The landlord has the key in the case of an emergency, but they have the only keys to the grow room area. The landlord is also instructed to leave a message on Bud's cell phone if there is an emergency. Bud's cell phone is registered under his Dutch relative's name. He also removes the battery from the cell phone when not in use. Cell phones act as a locating signal 24 hours a day. Removing the battery nullifies this feature.

Police are not always the biggest security risk for growers. Unfortunately, home invasions are becoming more commonplace. Secure deadbolts with strike plates are a must for all exterior doors. A big dog with big teeth is an excellent deterrent against home invasions. Either Bud or "J" are always at home and they do not talk about growing marijuana with anybody.

Bud's accounting background comes in very handy. He decided to keep their overhead less than 10 percent of (pound) selling price. For example, they are growing 6 pounds a month and selling each pound for $5000: (6 x 5000 = $30,000) $30,000 x 10% = $3000 expense allotment per month or $36,000 per year. Gross profit is figured on 6 pounds ($30,000) per month x 12 months = $360,000. They have $300,000 to split for the year plus all the smoke they need.

Once they were set up and harvested their first crop, they bought enough supplies for the next 6 months. They only bought an amount that would be easy to move. Their system does not require large amounts of new supplies.

Before starting to build the grow room, Bud asked "J": "Can we dismantle this entire room in less than 24 hours and remove all evidence of growing marijuana? Can we remove all traces of the grow room fast, just in case there is a problem and we have to move?" They planned their exact moves to dismantle the room. "Plan A" consisted of wrapping large plants in a paper sleeve and smaller plants are boxed for the move. They bought a bundle of 25 brown boxes the exact size they needed for the move.

There is also "Plan B" for a "knock and talk". A "knock and talk" is when the cops come to the front door *without* a search warrant and try to intimidate their target person into letting them search their home. Police have no right to enter a home unless someone agrees to let them in. No grower in their right mind would let the cops in without a search warrant that is signed by a judge! The police could return the next day with a bonafide search warrant. That's why they developed a plan to dismantle the grow room fast.

If they think the house is being watched and they cannot remove the plants, their plan is to burn the entire combustible contents of the grow room in the wood stove. They would pull all the plants, run them through a chipper and burn them, roots and all in the wood stove. They have a large pile of bone dry kindling to put in the stove to ignite the green plants. They would throw the hydroponic medium (clay pellets) in a large bin and pour dilute bleach over them to dissolve the roots. All traces of growing cannabis would go up in smoke or dissolve in bleach solution.

No scales, baggies, address books, phone numbers, cultivation manuals, marijuana magazines, or firearms are located at the grow house. These items are difficult to explain.

Bud and "J" were careful to keep construction generic with no custom shelves or tables. They keep building materials in whole pieces so they will be easy to move and reuse. Bud prefers screws, which are easy to drive and remove with an electric powered screwdriver. Nails require a noisy hammer to insert and a noisy, labor-intensive, messy process to extract. Nothing is permanent when you use screws. Everything goes together and comes apart quietly and easily.

Setting Up the Grow Room: Step-by-Step

The entire grow room should be set up in one to three days. This time frame includes setting up two 10 x 10-foot flowering rooms, and a 10 x 10-foot cloning/mother room, and taking clones.

Step One: Bud and "J" set up identical 10 x 10-foot flowering rooms next to each other in their basement. They also set up a 10 x 10-foot mother/clone room. There is a laundry room with a sink near the grow rooms.

Setting up the rooms requires few tools: a skill saw, fine-tooth jigsaw to cut Formica, 1/4" drill with a set of bits, black/white Visqueen plastic, electric screw driver, utility knife, tape measure, pencil, square, level and 1-1/2-inch and 4-inch sheet rock screws.

Noise can be a problem inside the grow room unless "sound board" is used. Sound board is a lightweight construction board available in 4' x 8' panels. Sound board can be cut with a sharp utility knife and one person can easily handle the lightweight sheets. White Formica, though a little expensive, can also be used as an easy-to-wash wall covering. Five or six sheet rock screws will fasten a sheet of 'sound board' to a wall securely.

Original walls are constructed from 2 x 4s on 36" centers. Next Bud and "J" put up sound board, insulation, more sound board, and black/white plastic or Formica. This construction technique is quick and easy to install with sheet rock screws and an electric screwdriver, much quieter than pounding with a hammer! They join the corners of the Formica together with aluminum tape. Use a fine-tooth jigsaw to cut Formica rather than a coarse-tooth blade which will break and tear the Formica.

These growers framed 2 x 4 walls on 36-inch centers to enclose the rooms. They covered the walls with sheet rock, sound board and Formica. They swept the rooms clean before mopping the concrete floor and wiping down the Formica walls with a 5 percent bleach solution.

Step Two: They also framed in a 10 x 10 mother/vegetative/clone room and installed a pre-hung, solid-core door and installed a deadbolt lock. The cloning area is located on a shelf in this room with two 40-watt fluorescent tubes (warm white and one cool white) overhead. They used "L" brackets to fasten the shelves to the wall. They also used adjustable chain to fasten the dual-bulb fluorescent fixture to the bottom of the top shelf.

Now both flowering rooms and the vegetative/mother/clone room are enclosed, secure and completely white.

Step Three: Bud and "J" use several large axial fans to keep the temperature at 75 degrees F during the day (65 degrees at night) and 50 percent relative humidity. The axial fans are plugged into thermostats that turn them on when temperatures rise above 75 degrees F. A 300 CFM axial fan exhausts air from each room through a length of 6 foot, 8-inch duct into a crawl space between the basement and the main floor.

Bud installed an ozone generator in the crawl space to neutralize odor during flowering. The ozone-treated air is vented out a duct he installed in the roof. See Chapter Two for more information on ozone generators.

An ozone generator is essential when growing a fragrant variety of marijuana. Bud sets up the ozone generator on a timer to be on for a few minutes every hour in the crawl space. Five minutes after the ozone generator shuts off, a vent fan changes the air in the crawl space. Ozone generators set up inside exhaust ducting must have enough time to treat the air. Ozone (O_3) must be in the same room as the smelly air for a minute or longer to neutralize the odor. After the odor is neutralized, the air can be evacuated.

Air that is pushed through an exhaust pipe or vent loses much velocity. The longer and smaller diameter the vent pipe, the less cubic feet per minute (CFM) of air that is able to move through. The shorter and wider the exhaust duct, the better. Bud's fan evacuates all the air out of the grow room in less than 5 minutes. For example, a room 10 x 10 x 8-feet = 800 cubic feet. 800 cu. ft. / 600 CFM = just over a minute to change air in room. The ducting should also run as straight as possible. Sharp (90-degree) corners restrict air flow and create back pressure on the fan, straining the motor and shortening its life.

Passive air flow is amazing. It works on the simple principle that hot air rises. Direct the hot air to an opening at the top of the grow room, and the heat escapes under its own power. If this heat is directed straight up a large vent, it moves quickly. If this movement is expedited with a slow-moving axial fan, large volumes of air are moved quietly and efficiently.

The best way to vent a room is straight up through the roof. This may require a little construction, but is often well worth the extra time and energy. Attach a "spinner" (spherical spinning fan) to the end of the duct, with a cap to protect it from the rain. The wind-activated spinning fan on the roof is designed to pull hot air out from the duct.

Fans vibrate and vibrations make noise. Bud secured their axial vent fan to the wall with thick rubber footings at each connection point to reduce noisy vibrations. The padded mounts for the axial vent fan virtually eliminated noise from vibrations.

Bud did not need an intake fan because the rooms are not tightly enclosed. New fresh air comes in through vents to the outside of the room and goes out the house via a dryer vent.

The flowering room has space on all sides to facilitate maintenance. Bud and "J" can easily reach in and touch every part of the garden. Air circulates better with space around the garden and air movement lessens problems.

Step Four: Bud sets up two oscillating fans to circulate air in and around each hydroponic system. Air circulation prevents air from stratifying around the leaves. The CO_2 around the leaves is used quickly; this air must be moved so more CO_2–rich air is available.

Step Five: Bud and "J" bought their first top-feed Nutrient Film Technique (NFT) hydroponic system from a hydroponic store. The system is simple and straight forward. They followed the manufacturer's directions to set up the hydroponic system. Once the system was set up, they filled the reservoir and turned it on to check for leaks. They found a couple of leaks and tightened the fittings until the leaks stopped.

Bud and "J" flower their plants in two top-feed NFT systems with 6" PVC tubes. Both hydroponic systems consist of two sets of six, 5-foot tubes lying next to one another on each side of a central reservoir. Three-inch holes drilled in the 6-inch PVC pipe on 7-inch centers hold Hydroclay-filled net pots of clones. Each 10-foot section of pipe contains 15 clones. Six (2 x 6) tubes x 15 clones = 90 plants.

This NFT system is similar to the original "AeroFlo" hydroponic garden developed by General Hydroponics™. It uses a 50-gallon reservoir with a manifold top-feed system. The nutrient is fed via spaghetti tubes into the top of each pot. It flows freely through the Hydroclay-filled containers 24 hours a day. The nutrient solution flows freely over the roots cascading down the tubes. This root zone environment is perfect for nutrient uptake. It offers ample air, free flowing nutrient solution and darkness.

Bud and "J" use General Hydroponics™ fertilizer and keep the *p*H of the nutrient solution at 6 – 6.2. The DS PPM (see Appendix for conversion to EC and CF) of the original tap water was near zero. They check the EC of the water before adding fertilizer. If the DS PPM is within 200 PPM of target, they add plain water. If the differential of the DS PPM is greater than 200, they add nutrient solution to bring it up to target level.

Step Six: It's difficult to say exactly what percentage of CO_2 increases yield. All Bud and "J" know is that when they quit using it, their yield fell by one pound per crop. They harvested 5 pounds without CO_2 instead of 6 pounds with CO_2. It was hot last summer and they turned off the CO_2 burner to keep the room cool. They are not sure why the yield decreased. It could have been the additional heat or the lack of CO_2. All they know is the harvest dipped and when they reintroduced CO_2, the yield went up. The experienced growers they know say that adding CO_2 is like night and day.

Step Seven: They hung three horizontal 1000-watt super metal halide lamps over each hydroponic system in the flowering rooms. They spaced the reflective hoods 1 – 2 inches apart. The bulbs are parallel to the shortest part of the table so the footprint of the light is shining most efficiently on the table. The fixtures are attached with strong hooks screwed into the joists above. Adjustable chain connects the hooks and the lighting fixtures.

Ballasts are located outside the grow room next to the relay box, between the flowering rooms. Electrical cords run along the ceiling and back to the ballasts so they stay out of the way.

Vegetative room lights are hung from hooks placed in the ceiling. Bud used lag bolts to secure a 2 x 4" across the joists of the ceiling. The hooks for the HPS fixtures are then screwed into the 2

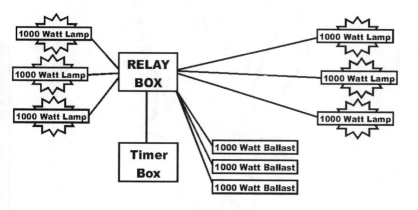

x 4". Two 400-watt metal halide lamps hang over a 4 x 6-foot area in the vegetative room. They secure the lamps from the hooks in the ceiling using heavy nylon cord. The rope is used to raise and lower the lamps, and the end of the cord is tied off to a cleat on the wall.

Step Eight: The Relay Box

Bud and "J" use three sets of ballasts to operate six lights. The ballasts are connected to a relay box. This ingenious box allows them to use the same transformers, capacitors and starters to operate two different sets of lamps. Three lamps operate from 6 AM until 6 PM. They turn off and the relay box turns on the other three halides in the other flowering room from 6 PM until 6 AM when the cycle is repeated.

Plants stretch less when they use halide lights. Using three 1000-watt halides so close together provides super intense light to

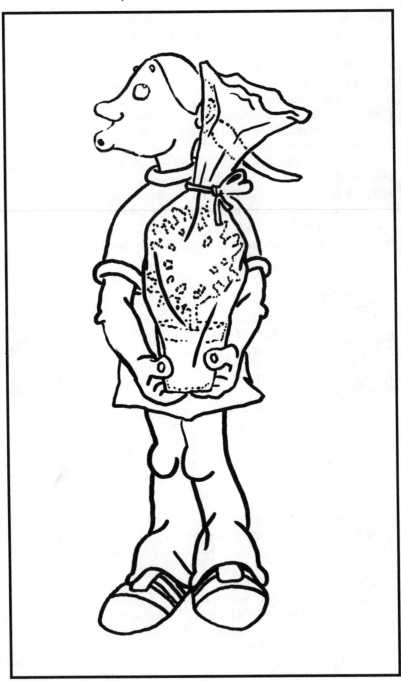

The easiest way to transport a plant is to wrap it in a paper sleeve to prevent damage.

the garden. However, the overall harvest weight is not increased. Big showy densely-packed buds with few large leaves, a manicurer's delight!

Step Nine: The growers installed an inexpensive hygrometer in each room so that they can increase ventilation when humidity climbs beyond 50 percent, to prevent plants from slow, sickly growth. They live in a northern climate with cool nights, and seldom have humidity problems.

Next, rooted clones are placed into the system, having been transplanted into net pots filled with "Hydro-Clay." The small rooted clones are huddled closely together under the lamp to receive intense light. Bud and "J" position the HIDs 3 feet above the garden until tender clones are acclimated to more intense light. They move the lamps 12 – 18 inches above the garden on the fourth or fifth day. When they grew seedlings, they kept the lamp at least 24 inches away until they were 6 inches tall. Then they moved the lamps 18 inches overhead.

Cloning

"Water stress will keep a clone from growing roots. I trim off all but the top three leaves and make sure the rooting medium is always evenly moist. Preventing clones from losing moisture through leaves ensures quick root growth," said "J" as he inspected a crop of rooting clones.

Oasis™ is "J's" favorite hydroponic medium to root clones. "J" likes Oasis™ cubes because they hold the right amount of water and air so roots grow evenly along the entire stem. "J" transplants Oasis™ cubes into Hydroclay pellets. He then installs a 1/8-inch spaghetti tube to feed nutrient solution to the top of the pots.

Clones are moved to the 12 hour flowering room just after roots are well established and start to grow fast and are about 6 inches tall. Clones are planted on seven-inch centers with 15 plants per 10-foot section of growing tube. A total of 90, 3 -1/2-inch holes are drilled in the tubes. Six, 10-foot tubes make up the garden illuminated by three 1000-watt horizontal HIDs.

(Day 1) Once mother plants are established, Bud begins taking clones from several mother plants kept in the vegetative room.

Step One: Bud's mothers are at least three months old and 24 inches tall. Five days before taking clones, he sets her in the laundry room sink and leaches the mother's 5-gallon pots with 15 gallons of water to wash out the nitrogen. Clones root better with low levels of nitrogen.

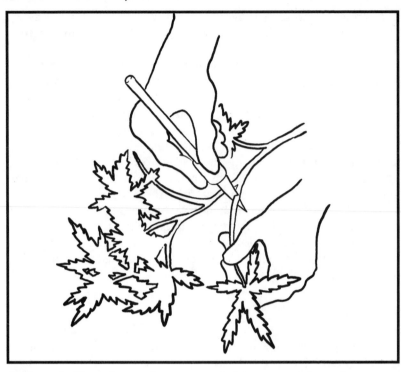

A sharp knife makes a clean cut and does not crush tender stems.

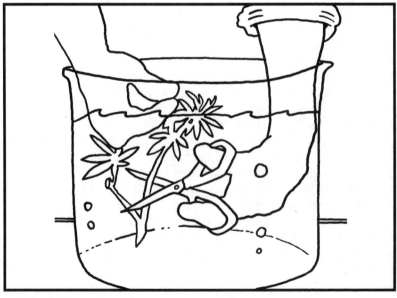

Avoid problems by taking cuttings under water.

Dip clones in root jell before placing in rooting medium.

Water rooted clones before transplanting.

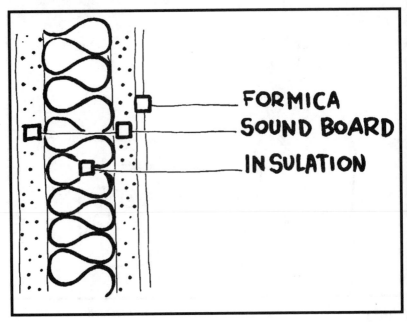

Layers of sound board, insulation, sound board, white Formica keep heat and sound inside the grow room.

This cloning chamber is compact, easy to build and efficient.

Air flow is impaired when the inside of the duct is not straight and smooth.

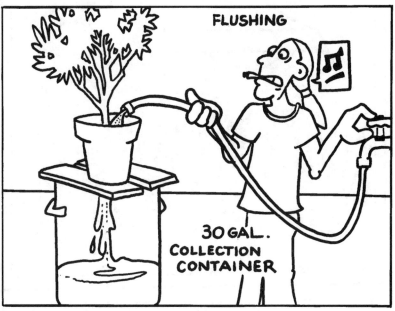

Leaching mother plants washes away nitrogen and makes clones root more easily.

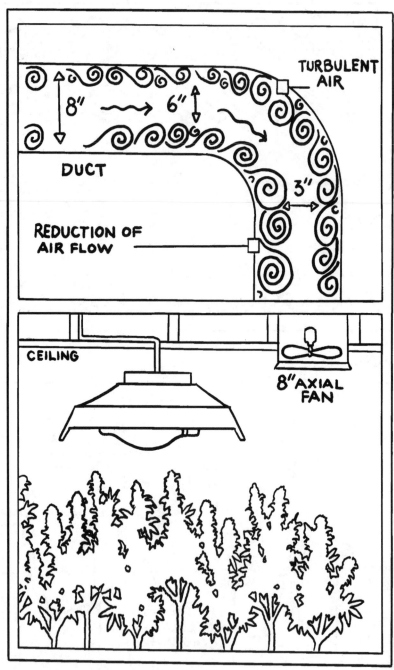

UPPER PANEL: *Much air flow is lost when ducting turns.*
LOWER PANEL: *Hot air flows upward naturally. Add a slow moving fan to increase the air flow.*

Step Two: Bud roots clones in small Oasis™ cubes. He sets out the number of Oasis™ cubes he plans to use and uses a chop stick to make the hole in the cube a little larger than the stem. The hole stops about a half inch from the bottom of the cube to allow for root growth.

Step Three: Bud cuts clones from older, lower branch tips. He uses a new single-edge razor blade to make a 45 degree cut across firm, healthy 1/8- to 1/4-inch-wide branches that are about 4 inches long. He is very careful to keep from smashing the end of the stem when making the cut. He trims off two or three sets of lower leaves so the stem will fit in the hole in the Oasis™ rooting cube. Ideal clones have two sets of leaves above the soil line and one or two sets of trimmed nodes below ground. Bud makes the cuts about a half inch below nodes.

Step Four: Bud dips the clone's stem in rooting hormone jell. When planting, he takes special care to keep a layer of rooting hormone jell around the stem when inserting it into the Oasis™ cube.

He immediately places the cut end in a rooting jell. Quick action here prevents an air bubble from lodging in the hole in the center of the stem, which would block the flow of fluids from the roots to the foliage. If this hole is blocked, the new cutting will die within 24 hours.

Another way to keep an air bubble from lodging in the stem, is to take the cutting under water. When a cutting is taken under water, no air is able to enter the hole in the stem.

Step Five: He waters the cubes after taking clones and lets excess nutrient solution drain off so no standing water is in the tray. He waters every few days with weak nutrient solution and the runoff drains away.

Step Six: Bud gives the rooting clones 24 hours of fluorescent light. He moves both of the flats under two 4-foot Vitalite fluorescent lamps. Bud puts clones 2-6 inches under Vitalite fluorescent tubes. Roots are growing out the sides of all the cubes in 14 to 21 days. Allowing clones to root longer allows them to establish strong healthy root growth.

Step Seven: He mists the new clones with water and puts a clear humidity tent over them to keep the humidity above 80 percent. He removes the transparent cover two or three times daily to mist with water and to give rooting clones fresh air.

Step Eight: In the winter, Bud adds a heating cable under the clone's bed to maintain the root zone temperature at 72 degrees.

Step Nine: Occasionally, a few cuttings wilt for a day or three before recouping. The growers trim the ends off leaves so they won't touch moist soil and rot. Less leaf area also holds water loss

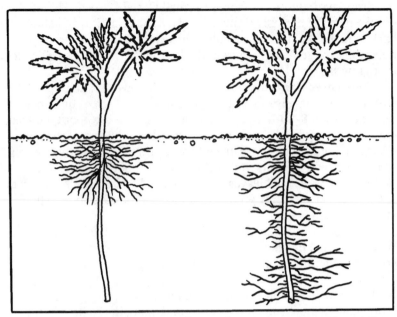

In poorly aerated growing mediums clones root along the surface. Roots will grow along the entire stem in well-aerated mediums.

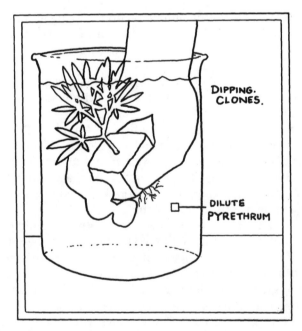

DIPPING. CLONES.

DILUTE PYRETHRUM

Baptizing clones in a bucket full of pyrethrum solution protects them from Spider Mites.

via the leaves to a minimum. Bud takes 50 cuttings and ends up with 45 healthy clones, each with a profuse and healthy white root system in two weeks.

Transplanting

(Day 15) Once clones have grown many white, fuzzy roots, the growers dip them in a pyrethrum solution before transplanting into 3-inch net pots filled with Hydroclay. Next, they put the clones under the two 400-watt halide lamps in a flood and drain table for 2 weeks before transplanting to the flowering room. Rockwool roots must have time to penetrate the cube before transplanting.

Spider Mites

Spider mites are the biggest pest problem Bud and "J" have had. Left unchecked, spider mites can devastate a garden in short order. Bud and "J" are clean freaks. I always stopped by to photograph their garden unannounced. I have visited many gardens: vegetable, flower, marijuana, formal and informal. Gardeners always say their garden could look better and I should have seen the last crop. Bud and "J" are no different, except that their garden is always spotless and packed with healthy plants. They dip clones in a pyrethrum solution twice before moving them to the flowering room, once after clones are rooted and again just before moving them to the flowering room. They rinse spray from plants by misting with water the next day. Clones are in the flowering room such a short time, mites scarcely

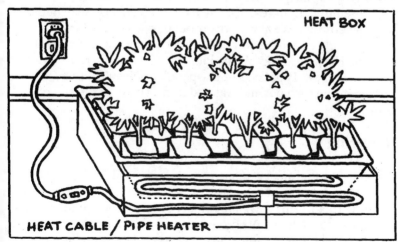

Inexpensive heat cables add warmth to the rooting clones, and speeds their growth.

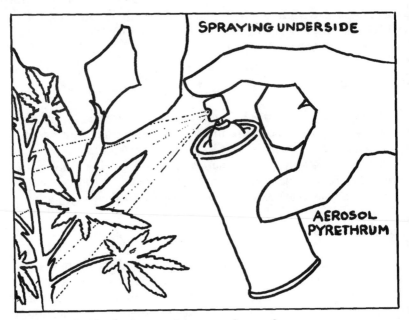

Misting individual plants with aerosol pyrethrum ensures spray gets under the leaves where mites live.

have time to infest them. If they see any mites, they spot spray with aerosol pyrethrum. They keep the nozzle at least a foot away from plants because spray is sub zero when it comes out of the nozzle. They also keep their garden free of disease. "J" always asks me if I have picked up any mites at another garden or nursery before he gives me permission to enter their grow rooms

"I used to fight mites off with Safer's Insecticidal Soap until we found pyrethrum. We always check out our plants and never let mites get out of hand," Bud said with the conviction of a man on a mission. He continued, "We had fungus gnats on the roots down inside the tubes. I applied 1/4 teaspoon of Wilson's Insect Dust (Diazanon) on each pot and watered it in. That was the end of them."

Flowering

(Day 36) Bud and "J" remove lower leaves and weak growth from the bottom six inches of the plants during transplanting to the flowering room. This weak growth does not get enough light when the plants grow tall. Plants grow much faster and stronger after the first two weeks and the stem girth increases. Irrigation lines fit easily under plucked plants, plus you can see that all the emitters are working.

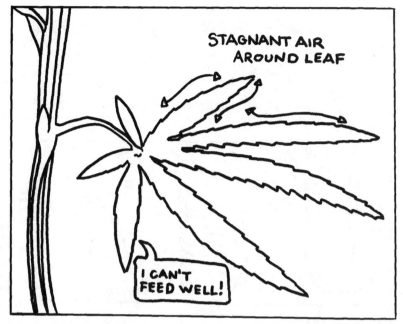

Carbon Dioxide depleted air remains around the leaves if it is not circulated.

After transplanting, smaller plants are set directly under the lamps and larger plants are set in tubes on the perimeter of the garden. Arranging smaller plants below bulbs helps all plants receive the maximum amount of light and retain an even garden profile. Plants can be moved the first week they are in the system. After that, roots are too long to move without damage.

Once the plants are transplanted into the flowering room, all they have to do is grow. They are fertilized and watered (fertigated) 24 hours a day. Some growers do not fertilize when the lights are off. Bud and "J" carefully lift up several baskets containing plants daily to inspect for brown rotting roots and fungus gnats. If roots show signs of browning or discoloration, they turn the water off at night. If the problem persists, they cut the irrigation schedule until roots have the proper amount of nutrient solution. (Do not attribute discoloration to a dark colored nutrient solution).

They replenish the nutrient tank with full strength solution daily until the desired PPM is met, then fresh water is added. If the dissolved solids PPM concentration goes beyond the desired point, plain water is added to top off the solution. The nutrient solution is kept between 65 and 69 degrees F., which keeps viruses at bay.

The nutrient solution could easily be warmed by heat from the lights if plants are small and don't shade tubes. Lights too close to

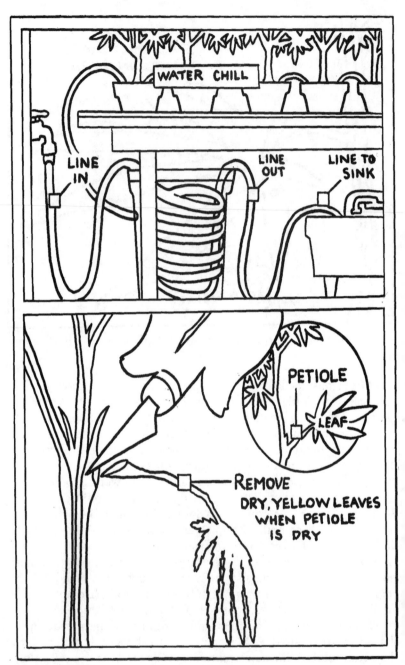

UPPER PANEL: *Fifty feet of spaghetti tubing carrying cold water is a perfect reservoir chiller.*
LOWER PANEL: *Cut off yellow leaves including the stem (petiole) to avoid rot.*

tubes heats them and the nutrient solution fast! If the temperature inside the tubes climbs beyond 69 degrees F., roots develop problems. Fungus gnats, about the size of aphids, will inhabit the roots, fungus (rot) and disease can become serious problems.

The reservoir is located on the cold concrete basement floor and stays between 70 to 75 degrees. Commercial growers keep the temperature of the nutrient solution below 69 degrees to help prevent deadly verticillium and pythium wilts. These deadly diseases are held in check and have difficulty growing at temperatures below 69 degrees. Bud and "J" effectively use SM 90, a fungicide from Western Water Farms, to keep these diseases in check.

The reservoir's temperature tends to climb during summer months. To keep the reservoir below 69 degrees, they submerge 50 feet of 1/4-inch spaghetti tubing in the reservoir. They attach one end to the faucet and run a trickle of cold water through the submerged hose. The other end of the hose drains back into the sink. The cold water running through the spaghetti tubing chills the reservoir to the desired temperature. They add tubing or increase cold water flow to lower the temperature of the reservoir. They cut tube length or decrease water flow to increase the temperature of the reservoir.

"Some grower's treat their nutrient solution with ozone to kill all waterborne diseases. I know it works, but we keep the temperature low and haven't had any problems" said Bud, and continued, "I know one grower that had root infestation of fungus gnats. He flushed the system three times in one day with hydrogen peroxide (H_2O_2). Then he flushed the system with water for an hour before he used a root sealant to protect the roots. He said there were handfuls of gnats that washed out of the system!"

Here is their fertilizer mix:

Cuttings are fertilized with General Hydroponics™
at the rate of 100-200 PPM – 3-1-1 - Flora + Micro
Vegetative plants are fertilized with General Hydroponics™
at the rate of 1000-1200 PPM – 3-1-1 - Flora + Grow + Micro
Flowering plants are fertilized with General Hydroponics™
at the rate of 600 PPM – 1-B/2-C - Bloom + Flora + Micro
The last 5 weeks they switch to General Hydroponics™
B + C Formula.
Last 2 weeks: flush with plain water,
to wash out any chemical fertilizer taste.

They clean and change the nutrient tank every seven days. To change the nutrient solution in the reservoir, they flush for half a

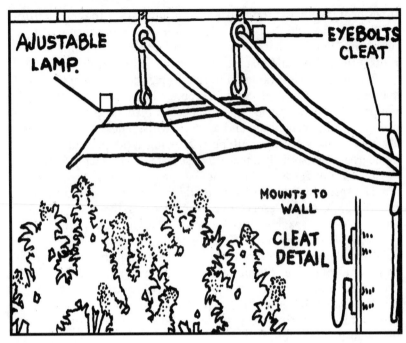

Run a nylon cord through eye bolts and tie to a cleat to hang the lights easily, and move them up and down as needed.

day with plain water, clean out the reservoir, and refill with plain water, flush again for an hour, then refill the reservoir with fresh nutrient solution.

"We clean the reservoir every week and keep adding full strength nutrient solution and water when the level runs low," said Bud. "Growing in soil was easy, all I had to do was look at the plants and make sure they were growing well. We haven't had any trouble with overfertilization, so we haven't worried very much about the concentration of fertilizer salts in the nutrient solution."

Bud uses a scrub brush to clean any salt buildup from the tank before replacing with fresh nutrient solution. He mixes the nutrient solution in 10-gallon batches so he can use pre-measured amounts of fertilizer and water. He adjusts the *p*H of the new nutrient solution in each batch before adding it to the tank. Bud and "J" check and adjust the *p*H of the nutrient solution daily.

They take cuttings when plants have been flowering for 3 weeks. The cuttings take 2 weeks to root and will be in the vegetative growth stage 3 weeks. The 5-week-old cuttings will be just right to move into the flowering room as soon as the other crop is harvested.

Harvest

(Day 92) "'Champagne' is a great variety to grow hydroponically. Most of the harvest is bud. When I was growing in soil, it took about a week to trim all the leaves from the buds. Now, in hydroponics it takes us only 5-6 hours to harvest and manicure an entire crop," said Bud with a smile.

BC growers love 'Champagne' because it emits virtually no odor when growing. Once cut and harvested, 'Champagne's' perfume permeates the air, and when properly cured, the smoke is smooth and potent.

Bud and "J" start picking off yellow leaves about two weeks before harvest. Any yellow leaf that has dried out all the way to the petiole (leaf stem) is removed. Leaves more than half damaged by insects, fungus, etc. are removed. They are careful to snip the entire leaf off at the main stem with scissors. Leaving the petiole (leaf stem) tends to attract fungus. Withholding fertilizer the last two weeks to remove fertilizer taste from buds also causes older leaves to turn yellow as harvest day approaches.

"Tall plants don't always produce good lower buds. Lower buds that don't get enough light are wispy. I clean all the feeble spindly growth from the bottom 6 inches of the plant when it has moved into flower. That way all the energy goes to the tops where there's light," explained Bud as he showed me a harvested two-ounce plant. "Our buds are bone dry and they get you high! That's what keeps customers coming back for more".

Do not remove green leaves from growing plants. Green leaves manufacture food so buds can grow big and strong. The only time to remove leaves is when they are yellow or diseased.

Every four weeks for the last 6 months Bud and "J" harvested a 5 – 6-pound crop from each flowering room. As soon as a crop is harvested, manicured and hanging on the drying lines, the system is completely scrubbed down by hand. No fertilizer salts are allowed to dry and build up in the system. Clean, fresh water is cycled in the system overnight, and new strong healthy clones are moved in by 6 PM the next day.

There are 90 plants in each room for a total of 180 flowering females. That's more than one plant for every square foot of growing space.

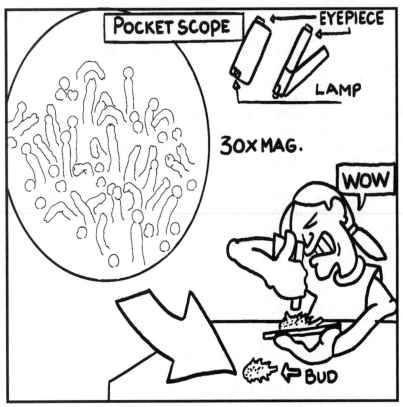

Resin glands are easy to see with a 30X microscope. Peak harvest is when half of the stalked resin glands are translucent and half turn amber.

Their goal is to harvest two ounces per plant. Nonetheless, they are limited by growing one-ounce and smaller plants.

In the last six months they have grown just over 30 pounds and should grow at least 60 pounds this year. That's a pretty good harvest for two 3000-watt flowering rooms and a vegetative/mother/clone room.

"We get right at two pounds per light in the flower room (one pound per 1000 watts per month) using this system. We got a lot of two-ounce plants, but we grew too many plants with half-ounce buds. This time we averaged better than one ounce of bud per plant overall. Our goal is to get two ounces per plant. Every crop we get a heavier harvest," said Bud as if trying to convince himself they could achieve the goal. (90 plants x 2 ounces = 180 ounces/16 = 11.25 pounds from one crop).

"The way I figure it, there are a couple of choices to increase yield. We have grown six crops in this system. The first time, we got 4.5 pounds under three 1000-watt halides. The second crop was a touch over five pounds and the last few crops have been six or more. I think we should be able to get two ounces per plant, but when I look at the garden, I wonder where is it going to fit? The garden is full of foliage now! Who knows, we might be close to maximum production with our room set up like it is now. We could continue to fine-tune this system to increase yield, or maybe it's better to change to 600-watt lamps and double our growing area," Bud proposed.

In Bud and "Js" garden, the 1000-watt halides hang very close to one another and bright light penetrates deep into the foliage. Bud thought about his soil gardening days. "We are getting about the same yield per light in this hydroponic system as I was when I was growing in soil. In soil, the plants and lights were spaced further apart."

The lights are spaced closer together and illuminate a smaller, more productive hydroponic tube garden. Does this mean that they could spread the lights out over a large hydroponic system and increase the growing area?

Three 1000-watt halides produce 345,000 initial lumens. Six 600-watt HP sodium lamps yield 540,000 initial lumens. They plan to change to 600-watt HP sodium lamps and add three more lamps (600 x 6 lamps = 3600 watts) in each room. They can add 600 watts, double growing area and increase the harvest.

"This hydroponic system is super productive, but I'm not sure if we can hit our target of two ounces per plant. I think our chances are better by changing to 600-watt lamps and doubling our growing area," says Bud, doing some math . . . "If we average 3/4-ounce on each table, we'll grow more than eight pounds and add only 600 watts!" (90 plants x 3/4 ounce = 67.50 ounces. Divide 67-1/2 ounces by 16 ounces = 4.2 pounds per table. If they have two tables, they can grow 8.4 pounds. (2 x 4.2 = 8.4 pounds).

They call the last 2 weeks of flowering "stinky weeks". That's why Bud and "J" are religious about keeping the smell contained in the flowering room. Drying buds in the flowering room contains the smell in the room. All the air vented into the crawl space is treated with ozone.

Female plants grow white pistils out of their seed bracts. The harvest is ready when more than 50 percent pistils turn dark but less than 75 percent are dark. This is the point when peak ripeness has been reached. In most indoor *indica/sativa* crosses, this peak is reached after 7 to 9 weeks of flowering under HID lights. Pure *sativa* buds can grow to unwieldy heights and ripen after 10 to 14 weeks of flowering.

The best way to discern peak ripeness of any marijuana is to look at it with a 30X hand-held microscope. A quick peek through the scope will reveal the resin glands located on the buds and leaves. You will see different types of resin glands (trichomes). The capitate stalked glands are where the psychoactive THC (tetra-hydro cannabinol) is located. The biggest concentration of THC is found within the base of the bulb on the capitate trichomes. A high concentration of capitate-stalked trichomes indicates good dope.

Peak ripeness is reached when just over half of the capitate-stalked trichomes change from a light translucent color to amber. The capitate-stalked trichomes past peak ripeness are dark amber with misshapen bulbs.

To harvest, Bud and "J" clip stems of the leaf-bare plants below branch forks at nodes forming a hook. They remove large fan leaves as they collect the branches. Once a dozen or so branches are collected, they are manicured with small scissors. They hang the manicured bud-laden branches from the natural hook on drying lines. Leaves are sorted into paper shopping bags and made into hash later. An oscillating fan keeps the air circulating around the tops and reduces fungus attacks. A heater is added to warm and dry the air when outdoor temperatures are cool.

Buds are dry enough to sell when the stem breaks on a bud or growers can keep a joint lit. In 4 – 10 days, depending on outdoor weather, the buds are dry enough to smoke. The branches are removed from the drying lines and placed into paper grocery bags to finish drying. If buds get too dry on the outside and are still wet on the inside, they are placed in an open plastic bag. The plastic bag helps moisture equalize between the stem and foliage so the buds will dry evenly. They might need to be placed back in the paper bag to dry a little more after they come out of the plastic bag. Buds are always handled carefully to prevent damage to resin glands.

They clean the hydroponic system immediately after harvest and do not wait until fertilizer salts dry and harden. The system is much more difficult to clean once fertilizer salts have hardened. If salts build up and the system is reused, the nutrient solution will be imbalanced and the irrigation system tends to clog.

Twenty-four hours after harvest, after the hydroponic tube system is clean, they move new clones in for the next crop!

Bud's Bonus Garden

"Before "J" and I got this house, I had another small place with two flowering rooms. One room would bud out every month. I had four HP sodium lamps in each room, a total of 8000 watts," Bud explained.

"I grew 20 plants in each room. Each plant yielded an average of 5 ounces by the end of an 8-week bud cycle. I consistently harvested 6 to 6-1/2 pounds of bud every eight weeks. The plants were always healthy and strong. I would transplant clones that had rooted for two weeks into two-gallon pots and grow them for 3 – 4 weeks. At harvest they were about three feet tall, strong and bushy," continued Bud.

"I transplanted clones into five-gallon pots full of Sunshine #4 mix when I flowered them. Seven weeks later, nice, thick, juicy, resin-squirting buds were ready to harvest."

"I was growing the same variety, 'Champagne', that we are growing now. It is my favorite variety and I know how to grow it. When I was growing in soil, 'Champagne' produced a lot of leaf. I mean a lot of leaf. Too much leaf compared to the amount of bud. Clipping and manicuring buds was a long and tedious process. I would have to hire 5 guys to clip for two days. That's 40 hours of manicuring to get 6 pounds. It cost me half a pound just to pay the trimmers! Besides constantly removing yellow leaves, I had to get rid of 10 bags of soil after every harvest," complained Bud loudly.

"I learned how to grow in soil, but I don't miss all the watering and bending over to move water-soaked grow bags. I'm a convert to hydroponics. It has been less work and easier for me. Now I feel comfortable with hydroponics and let me tell you it's a lot less work to set up, take care of, and harvest," Bud said with a smile and continued, "We are thinking about putting some plants in soil around the perimeter to soak up the extra unused light."

Construction Supplies
Approximate Cost

Bleach	$5
Board, 2 x 4s to frame 10 x 10 rooms	$30
Board, 3/4" plywood – 2' x 3'	$12
Cable ties to bundle wire	$5
CO_2 generator	$300
Deadbolt lock	$20
Door handle	$10
Drill, electric and drill bits	$0
Ducting, flexible/expandable 8"	$30
Fan, 4, 300 CFM axial vent	$200
Fan, 3 – 16-inch circulation fans	$90
Formica, 4 x 8-foot sheets	$90
Hardware (hooks, screws, chain, etc.)	$10
Hydroponic systems, two, NFT tube systems	$1500
Hygrometer	$10
Jig Saw	$40
Level	$10
Lights, flowering rooms – six 1000-watt metal halides	$1400
Lights, vegetative room – two 400-watt metal halides	$500
Ozone generator	$300
Plastic, Black/white Visqueen for walls	$50
Pump-up quart spray bottle	$15
Relay box	$200
Saw, electric circular	$30
Screwdriver, electric	$30
Screws, sheet rock 1-1/2 and 4-inch	$10
Sheet rock, 4 pieces of 4' x 8' x 1/2"	$20
Solid-core pre-hung door	$100
Square	$10
Staples for stapler	$5
Tape measure	$10
Timer for lights	$30
Two pulleys and nylon cords to hang fluorescent fixture	$10
Thermostat	$80
Utility knife	$5
Total	**$5,167**

Grow Supplies

Fertilizer – General Hydroponics™	$20
Flats – 2, 10" x 20" x 2" with drainage and humidity tents	$5
Hose, 50-feet 1/8-inch tubing to cool reservoir	$30
Microscope, 30X	$50
pH meter	$30
Pesticide, Pyrethrum aerosol	$10
Pruners	$20
Rooting hormone jell	$10
Water can – 2-gallon	$20

Total   **$5362**

Electricity:
(also see chart in Appendix)

6000-watts (6) x 12 hrs x 30 days = 2160 kilowatt-hours (KWH)
800-watts (0.8) x 18 hrs x 30 days = 432 kilowatt-hours
2160 + 432 = 2592 kilowatt hours per month
2592 x $0.10 (cost of KWH) = **$259.20** increase in monthly
electricity bill if electricity costs $0.10 per KWH.

$5362 setup cost
$259.20 - 30-day electricity bill
$259.20 - 30-day electricity bill
$5880.40 Total cost to grow first crop

$5880/96 ounces = **$61.25** per ounce for the first crop
$700/96 ounces = **$7.29** per ounce for each additional crop

Garden Calendar

1. Take clones	January 1
2. Transplant to 2-gallon pots (18 hrs)	January 15
3. Induce flowering (12 hrs)	February 5
4. Change to flowering fertilizer	February 5
5. Harvest	March 19
6. Take clones	January 22
7. Transplant to 2-gallon pots (18 hrs)	February 5
8. Induce flowering (12 hrs)	February 26
9. Change to flowering fertilizer	February 26
10. Harvest	April 9
11. Take clones	Feb. 12
12. Transplant to 2-gallon pots (18 hrs)	Feb. 26
13. Induce flowering (12 hrs)	March 19
14. Change to flowering fertilizer	March 19
15. Harvest	April 30
16. Take clones	March 5
17. Transplant to 2-gallon pots (18 hrs)	March 19
18. Induce flowering (12 hrs)	April 9
19. Change to flowering fertilizer	April 9
20. Harvest	May 21

Growing Statistics

Yield:	6 pounds every 4 weeks
Lbs/1000-w/30 days:	1
Grams/watt/30 days:	0.45
Clone room:	Root 200 clones 21 days
Part of vegetative	four, 40-watt Vitalite fluorescent
room	tubes
	24 hours per day
	Oasis™ cubes
Vegetative room:	Grow 190 plants for 2 weeks
10 x 12 feet	two 400-watt metal halides
	18 hours per day
	three-inch net pots of Hydroclay
Flowering room:	Grow 180 plants for 8 weeks
12 x 27 feet	six (3 + 3) 1000-watt metal halides
	12 hours per day
	three-inch net pots of Hydroclay in
	NFT tubes
Harvest:	180 (90 + 90) 2 – 3-foot tall plants
	Average weight 1+ ounces each.

Monthly electricity cost (@ *$0.10 per KWH*)**:** $259.20
First crop cost: $5880 total (**$61.25** per ounce)
Next crop cost: $700 (**$7.25** per ounce)

• **To downsize their garden by 50 percent,** Bud and "J" would use two 40-watt fluorescent tubes, two 400-watt metal halides (or HPS) lamps and three 1000-watt metal halides (or HP sodiums). They would also use one instead of two flowering rooms. They would not need the relay to operate two sets of lights. Their construction expenses would be about half because they would set up only one flowering room. Bud and "J" would have to work half as hard and their harvest would be cut in half. Growing **Statistics**

Yield:	6 pounds every 8 weeks
Lbs/1000-w/30 days:	1
Grams/watt/30 days:	0.45
Clone room:	Root 100 clones 21 days Part of
vegetative	two, 40-watt Vitalite fluorescent
room	tubes 24 hours per day
	Oasis™ cubes
Vegetative room:	Grow 95 plants for 2 weeks
10 x 12 feet	one 400-watt metal halide
	18 hours per day

	three-inch net pots of Hydroclay
Flowering room:	Grow 90 plants for 8 weeks
12 x 27 feet	three 1000-watt metal halides
	or HPS
	12 hours per day
	three-inch net pots of Hydroclay in
	NFT tubes
Harvest:	90, 2 – 3 -foot tall plants
	Average weight 1 + ounces each.

Monthly electricity cost *(@ $0.10 per KWH)*: $129.60
First crop cost: $3200 total (**$80.75** per ounce)
Next crop cost: $250 (**$5.20** per ounce)

• **To downsize their garden by 70 percent,** Bud and "J" would use two 40-watt fluorescent tubes, one 400-watt metal halide (or HPS) lamps and three 600-watt HP sodiums. They would also use one instead of two flowering rooms. They would not need the relay to operate two sets of lights. Their construction expenses would be about half because they would set up only one flowering room. Bud and "J" would have to work half as hard and their harvest would be cut in half.

Growing Statistics

Yield:	3 pounds every 8 weeks
Lbs/1000-w/30 days:	1
Grams/watt/30 days:	0.45
Clone room:	Root 100 clones 21 days
Part of vegetative tubes	two, 40-watt Vitalite fluorescent
room	24 hours per day
	Oasis™ cubes
Vegetative room:	Grow 95 plants for 2 weeks
10 x 12 feet	one 400-watt metal halide
	18 hours per day
	three-inch net pots of Hydroclay
Flowering room:	Grow 90 plants for 8 weeks
12 x 27 feet	three 600-watt HP sodiums
	12 hours per day
	three-inch net pots of Hydroclay in NFT tubes
Harvest:	90, 2 – 3 -foot tall plants
	Average weight 0.6 ounces each.

Monthly electricity cost *(@ $0.10 per KWH)*: **$88.97**
First crop cost: $2584 total (**$80.75** per ounce)
Next crop cost: $1000 (**$7.81** per ounce)

Chapter Six
Illuminating Facts of Light

Too many growers hang up a HID light to grow plants and that's the last they think about light. But which is the best light and how is the intensity best managed for optimum results? With the proper lamp and reflective hood, most growers could increase light in their room 10 – 40 percent and use the same amount of electricity. That's more light, more plants, bigger bud and a heavier harvest for the same electric bill!

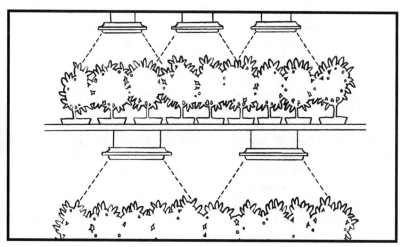

Three 600-watt lamps and two 1000-watt lamps over a garden.

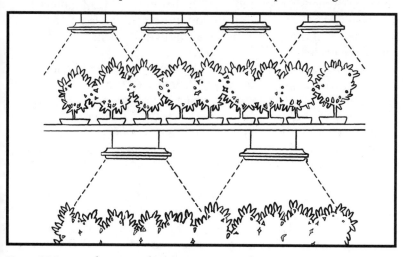

Four 600-watt lamps and two 1000-watt lamps over a garden.

Metal halide and high pressure (HP) sodium light manufacturers include Philips, General Electric, Iwasaki, Venture, Osram/Sylvania and SunMaster. Many growers are partial to one brand over another and swear the bulbs they use grow the best dope in the world. What they don't know is that manufacturers buy and use the same components, often manufactured by competitors. Sylvania invented the High Intensity Discharge (HID) technology in the 1970s. Sylvania soon licensed this technology to other corporations. Manufacturing HID bulbs requires several very expensive processes that are completed at only a handful of factories. Often, these factories sell bulb components to one another even though they compete for the same customers' business. Most often competing companies' bulbs have the exact same technical specifications.

Bulbs for specific purposes (such as the HP sodium Son Agro by Phillips) produce a little more blue in the spectrum which helps prevent plants from stretching and becoming leggy. Different conversion bulbs such as the White Ace (Iwasaki) or the White Lux (Venture) produce a metal halide spectrum and can be used in an HPS ballast. The HP sodium to metal halide conversion bulbs include the Sunlux Super Ace and Ultra Ace (Iwasaki) or the Retrolux (Philips). These allow you to use a metal halide ballast and get the spectrum of a HP sodium lamp. You trade lumen-per-watt efficiency for the convenience of using these bulbs.

New bulbs are entering the market every year. It is difficult to keep up with all the new bulbs from different countries. I always look at the technical specifications to find the "initial lumens-per-watt" as the major comparison between bulbs.

Lumens from HID lamps are a substitute for natural sunlight. The more lumens a plant receives, the better it grows. Lumens diminish very quickly. So it is important to keep the lamp 18" to 24" from the top of the garden so the bright light (lumens) is able to spread out evenly.

Metal halide lamps produce a full, even spectrum of light. The light shines clear and is virtually the same spectrum as natural sunlight. They contain the proper balance of both blue and red light plants need to keep them growing as they would under natural sunlight. Halides are preferred by some growers for vegetative growth, especially for mother plants. Halides most commonly used by growers are the "super" version that supplies up to 10 percent more light than standard types. These bulbs can be either clear or phosphor coated. The coated halides bear a little more reddish light and yield about 4 percent less light than their clear counterpart. Metal halides are also classified as to their vertical or horizontal operating capacity. They are rated to operate base up (BU) with the threads of the bulb toward the ceiling, horizontal (H) or universal

(U), which can function in any position. Note: universal bulbs produce fewer lumens than horizontal bulbs. You can always tell a horizontal metal halide bulb; it requires a specific horizontal socket, which is usually yellow, and the bulb has a small pin on the threaded base that locks into a notch in the special socket.

Many successful growers use exclusively HP sodium lamps that produce more light per watt of electricity than metal halides. A 1000-watt super metal halide produces 115,000 initial lumens compared to 140,000 initial lumens produced by a 1000-watt HP sodium bulb. That's about 20 percent more light for the same amount of electricity. The sodium also produces more light in the yellow/orange spectrum. This light spectrum makes most marijuana varieties stretch a little more between internodes. A plant that's a little taller stretches is a small price to pay for 20 percent more lumens. Smart growers prefer HP sodium lamps. They are brighter, last longer and perform equally well in either horizontal or vertical burning positions. They offer the brightest light for the buck.

Flower buds form tighter under brighter light. You can see a good example in the color section. The 'Champagne' variety (see photos 40 – 48 in color section) was grown with more overall lumens (3, 1000-watt phosphor-coated halides over a 6 x 10-foot area) and the other 'Champagne' plants (see photo 19 in color section) are grown with about 30 percent fewer lumens. Notice how much tighter the buds are in the 6 x 10-foot garden.

Also keep lights close enough to plants so they won't stretch to find more light; it will cost lumens. You can also mix both types of bulbs, HP sodium and super metal halides, to keep plants from stretching. The ratio of one metal halide to four or five HP sodium lamps will give you enough blue light in the spectrum to keep plants from stretching. If you decide to mix halide and HP sodium bulbs, hang the metal halide fixture higher than the sodium lamps so that blue light from the halide reaches the entire garden. You can also purchase a four-arm Sun Circle™ and install three HP sodium bulbs and one super metal halide for best results. With a Sun Circle™, all of the plants receive the same spectrum of light.

According to the Sensi Seed Bank of Holland, one 400-watt lamp produces enough light for one square meter, or a little over one square yard (almost 10 square feet). Remember, this advice comes from Holland where they use super efficient Philips or PL reflective hoods and 400-watt HP sodium or 430-watt Son Agro sodium bulbs. This can easily be misinterpreted in North America to mean *any* 400 watt lamp with *any* reflective hood will illuminate a 3-foot by 3-foot area effectively. Wrong!

Watt for watt, except for the 600-watt, *any* HP sodium bulb is a 20 percent better value than *any* super metal halide. The 600-watt

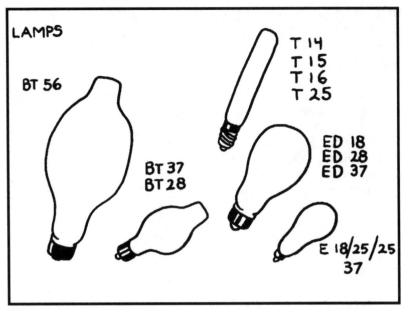

HID lamps – 150, 400, 430, 600, 1000 watts are available in different bulb sizes and shapes.

HP sodium is 25 percent better. You can increase light output by as much as 40 percent by choosing the right reflective hood. Couple this 40 percent with 20-25 percent more light from a HP sodium and you have up to 60 percent more light for the same amount of electricity!

I read many claims from reflective hood manufacturers. None of the information made sense to me because there was little comparative hard data to their claims. I decided to make a few tests of my own. I bought a good light meter and set up a room to test different reflectors.

I set up a room, and painted it black so there would be virtually no reflected light. I marked out a 12-inch square grid on the floor. I suspended each lamp and reflective hood measured 3 feet above the floor in the center of the grid. I let the lamp warm up and measured how much light hit the floor on each square foot. The results were enlightening.

I carefully took foot-candle readings from each meeting point on the grid and entered the information on a computer spreadsheet. I loaded this information into Microsoft Excel for Windows 95 and used the graph option to make graphs of the light output.

Not all hoods reflect equally. Hoods that performed the best had a pebble or hammer specular finish, or anodized aluminum or white reflective surface. Glossy white tended to create hot spots under the bulb. Shiny mirror finishes performed the absolute worst. Horizontal hoods reflected more light than vertical reflectors.

Horizontal hoods with a dual parabolic design normally reflected the most light the most evenly. A smooth dual parabolic design is completely different from a hood with the dual parabola formed with angles. The angles bent into the hood reflect light unevenly. The dual parabolic shape of the Adjust-A-Shade (AKA Adjust-A-Wing) is one of the best. Small dual parabolic hoods reflect light unevenly and tend to have a hot spot below the bulb.

These tests prove you get more light from some hoods than others. How much does this cost in dollars and sinsemilla? Beaucoup! For example, if you are paying $0.10 US for a kilowatt of electricity and your 1000-watt HP sodium lamp is on 12 hours for 30 days it costs $36 a month to operate. We know that a well-designed horizontal hood reflects up to 40 percent more light than a vertical cone hood. For the sake of this example, let's say the horizontal hood reflects 100 percent light and the cone hood reflects 60 percent as much light (or 40 percent less than 100 percent). To find out how much more it costs to use a cone hood take 60 percent of $36 to equal $21.60. It costs $14.40 ($36 - $21.60 = $14.40) more every month to operate a cone hood!

If the best horizontal hood costs $50, this means enough money could be saved from the electric bill in 3.5 months (3.5 x $14.40 = $50.40) to pay for a new horizontal hood which produces 40 percent more light. Imagine how much more dope could be grown with 40 percent more light.

This example only looks at a few reflective hoods. Smart growers buy a light meter, (cost $30 to $200) to measure the light in their gardens and make decisions based on actual information collected.

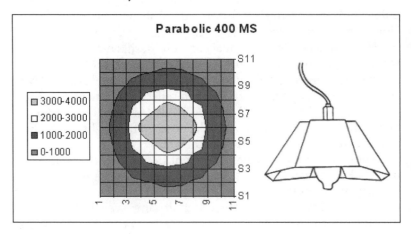

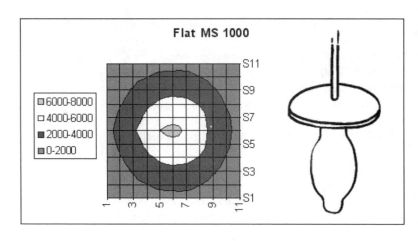

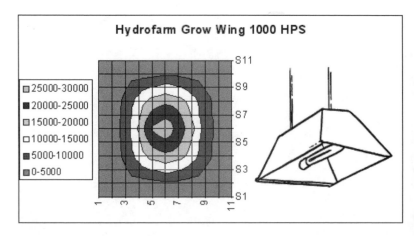

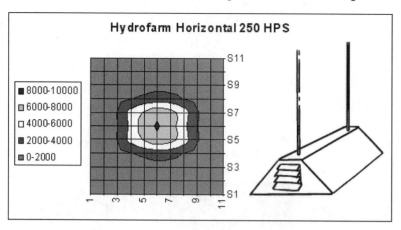

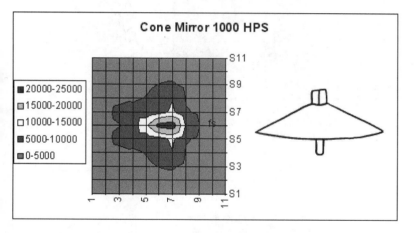

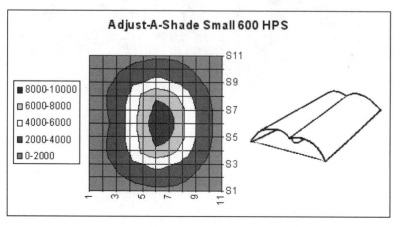

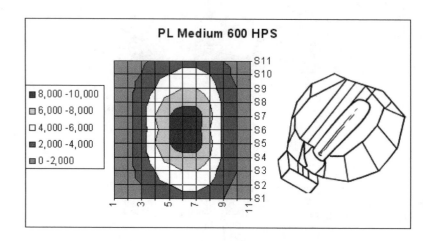

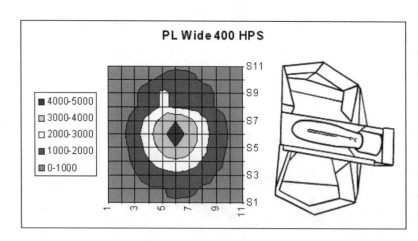

Appendix

Humidity

Relative humidity is the ratio between the amount of moisture in the air and the greatest amount of moisture the air could hold at the same temperature. The hotter it is, the more moisture air can hold; the cooler it is, the less moisture the air can hold. When the temperature in a grow room drops, the humidity climbs and moisture condenses. For example, a 800 cubic foot (10' x 10' x 8') grow room will hold a maximum of about 14 ounces of water when the temperature is 700 and relative humidity is at 100 percent. When the temperature is increased to 1,000 the same room will hold about 56 ounces of moisture at 100 percent relative humidity. That's four times as much moisture! Where does this water go when the temperature drops?

A 10 x 10 x 8' (800 cubic feet) grow room can hold:

> 4 oz. of water at 320
> 7 oz. of water at 500
> 14 oz. of water at 700
> 18 oz. of water at 800
> 28 oz. of water at 900
> 56 oz. of water at 1,000

Relative humidity increases when the temperature drops at night. The more temperature variation, the greater the relative humidity variation. Supplemental heat or extra ventilation may be necessary at night if temperatures fluctuate more than 15 degrees F.

Testing EC, CF and DS PPM

A nutrient tester's main function is to measure Electrical Conductivity (EC), in solution. EC is the ability of a solution to carry an electrical current. Dissolved Ionic Salts create electrical current in solution, the main constituent of hydroponic solutions is ionic salts.

EC s commonly measured in either (a) Millisiemens per Centimeter (MS/CM) or (b) Microsiemens per Centimeter (US/CM).

One Millisiemen/CM = 1000 Millisiemens/CM

PPM testers actually measure in EC but then show a conversion reading in PPM. Unfortunately, the two scales (EC and PPM) are not directly related, because each type of salt gives a different electronic discharge reading. A standard is selected which assumes "so much EC means so much salt" in a nutrient in the solution. The result gives only an idea of the PPM in the nutrient solution.

It gets worse. Nutrient tester manufacturers use different standards to convert to the PPM reading.

1. Hanna	1MS/CM = 500 PPM
2. Eutech	1MS/CM = 640 PPM
3. New Zealand Hydro.	1MS/CM = 700 PPM

PPM readings may be confusing. Below is an easy-reference chart with the conversions listed. You will see by the scale of the PPM reading you obtain from your meter can gave quite drastic differences depending on which brand of meter you use.

Conversion scale from PPM/CF.

EC MS/CM0.5	Hanna 0.64	Eutech 0.70	Truncheon 0	CF
0.1	50 ppm	64 ppm	70 ppm	1
0.2	100 ppm	128 ppm	140 ppm	2
0.3	150 ppm	192 ppm	210 ppm	3
0.4	200 ppm	256 ppm	280 ppm	4
0.5	250 ppm	320 ppm	350 ppm	5
0.6	300 ppm	384 ppm	420 ppm	6
0.7	350 ppm	448 ppm	490 ppm	7
0.8	400 ppm	512 ppm	560 ppm	8
0.9	450 ppm	576 ppm	630 ppm	9
1.0	500 ppm	640 ppm	700 ppm	10
1.1	550 ppm	704 ppm	770 ppm	11
1.2	600 ppm	768 ppm	840 ppm	12
1.3	650 ppm	832 ppm	910 ppm	13
1.4	700 ppm	896 ppm	980 ppm	14
1.5	750 ppm	960 ppm	1050 ppm	15
1.6	800 ppm	1024 ppm	1120 ppm	16
1.7	850 ppm	1088 ppm	1190 ppm	17
1.8	900 ppm	1152 ppm	1260 ppm	18
1.9	950 ppm	1260 ppm	1330 ppm	19
2.0	1000 ppm	1280 ppm	1400 ppm	20
2.1	1050 ppm	1344 ppm	1470 ppm	21
2.2	1100 ppm	1408 ppm	1540 ppm	22
2.3	1150 ppm	1472 ppm	1610 ppm	23
2.4	1200 ppm	1536 ppm	1680 ppm	24
2.5	1250 ppm	1600 ppm	1750 ppm	25
2.6	1300 ppm	1664 ppm	1820 ppm	26
2.7	1350 ppm	1728 ppm	1890 ppm	27
2.8	1400 ppm	1792 ppm	1960 ppm	28
2.9	1450 ppm	1856 ppm	2030 ppm	29
3.0	1500 ppm	1920 ppm	2100 ppm	30
3.1	1550 ppm	1984 ppm	2170 ppm	31
3.2	1600 ppm	2048 ppm	2240 ppm	32

Electricity Expenses

12-hour Days			18-hour Days	
$US	Day	Month	Day	Month
$0.02	0.24	7.20	0.36	10.80
$0.03	0.36	10.80	0.54	16.20
$0.04	0.48	14.40	0.72	21.60
$0.05	0.60	18.00	0.90	27.00
$0.06	0.72	21.60	1.08	32.40
$0.07	0.84	25.20	1.26	37.80
$0.08	0.96	28.80	1.44	43.20
$0.09	1.08	32.40	1.62	48.60
$0.10	1.20	36.00	1.80	54.00

Conversion to Metric

When You Know	Multiply by	To Find
Length		
millimeters	0.04	inches
centimeters	0.39	inches
meters	3.28	feet
kilometers	0.62	miles
inches	25.40	millimeters
inches	2.54	centimeters
feet	30.48	centimeters
yards	0.91	meters
miles	1.16	kilometers

Area

square centimeters	0.16	square inches
square meters	1.20	square yards
square kilometers	0.39	square miles
hectares	2.47	acres
square inches	6.45	square centimeters
square feet	0.09	square meters
square yards	0.84	square meters
square miles	2.60	square kilometers
acres	0.40	hectares

Volume

milliliters	0.20	teaspoons
milliliters	0.60	tablespoons
milliliters	0.03	fluid ounces
liters	4.23	cups
liters	2.12	pints
liters	1.06	quarts
liters	0.26	gallons
cubic meters	35.32	cubic feet
cubic meters	1.35	cubic yards
teaspoons	4.93	milliliters
tablespoons	14.78	milliliters
fluid ounces	29.57	milliliters
cups	0.24	liters
pints	0.47	liters
quarts	0.95	liters
gallons	3.790	liters

Mass and Weight

grams	0.035	ounce
kilograms	2.21	pounds
ounces	28.35	grams
pounds	0.45	kilograms

1 inch (in.) = 25.4 millimeters (mm)
1 foot (12 in.) = 0.3048 meters (m)
1 yard (3 ft) = 0.9144 meters
1 mile = 1.60937 kilometers
1 square inch = 645 square millimeters
1 square foot = 0.0929 square meters
1 square yard = 0.8361 square meters
1 square mile = 2.59 square kilometers

Liquid Measure Conversion

1 pint (UK) = 0.56824 liters
1 pint dry (US) = 0.55059 liters
1 pint liquid (US) = 0.47316 liters
1 gallon (UK) (8 pints) = 4.5459 liters
1 gallon dry (US) = 4.4047 liters
1 pint liquid (US) = 3.7853 liters

1 ounce = 28.3495 grams
1 pound (16 ounces) = 0.453592 kilograms

1 gram = 15.4325 grains
1 kilogram = 2.2046223 pounds

1 millimeter = 0.03937014 inches (UK)
1 millimeter = 0.03937 inches (US)
1 centimeter = 0.3937014 inches (UK)
1 centimeter = 0.3937 inches (US)
1 meter = 3.280845 feet (UK)
1 meter = 3.280833 feet (US)
1 kilometer = 0.6213722 miles

Celsius to Fahrenheit

Celsius temp. x (9/5 = 32) = Fahrenheit
Fahrenheit temp. -32, 5/9 x remainder = Celsius

Light Conversion

1 footcandle = 10.76 lux
1 lux = 0.09293
Lux = 1 lumen/square meters

Index

Notes

Notes

A list of interesting publications from
Marlin's Book Distribution:

ABC of NFT $39.95
Basic Hydroponics 13.95
Beginning Hydroponics 13.95
Best of Sinsemilla Tips 19.95
Build You Own Greenhouse 12.95
Canamo Magazine (Spanish) 7.95
Closet Cultivator 16.95
Commercial Hydroponics 18.95
Cogollo Magazine (Spanish) 4.95
Emperor Wears No Clothes 24.95
Gardening Under Lights Video 29.95
Growing Edge Magazine 5.00
Grow! Magazine (German/English) 7.95
Hanf (German) 7.95
HASHISH! (NEW) R. Clarke 29.95
Home Hydroponics 13.95
Hydroponic Crop Production 24.95
Hydroponics Explained Video 29.95
Hydroponics Step-By-Step Video 29.95
Hydroponic Food Production 49.95
Hydroponic Hot House 16.95
Joint Rolling Handbook 9.95
Marijuana Botany 21.95
Marijuana Chemistry 19.95
Manual del Cultivo (Spanish) 19.95
Marijuana-High Yield 19.95
Marijuana Grower's Guide Deluxe 19.95
Marijuana Grower's Guide Deluxe-Spiral 23.95
Marijuana Herbal Cookbook 14.95
Marijuana Insider's Guide 19.95
Marijuana in Cool Climate 14.95
Marijuana Flower Forcing 16.95
Marijuana Hydroponics 16.95
Mundo High Magazine (Spanish) 7.95
Marijuana Question? Ask Ed 19.95
Mushroom Cultivator 29.95
Organic Pest Control 12.95
Practical Hydroponics Magazine 6.95
Rasta Cookbook 14.95
Sea of Green Book 19.95
Sea of Green Video 29.95
Sea of Green Video Vol. 2 .... 29.95
Secret Life of Plants 19.95
Shattered Lives: Portraits From America's Drug War 19.95
Sinsemilla Technique 24.95
Weed World Magazine (UK) 9.95

Also Available from Marlin's Book Distribution:

Marijuana Outdoors: Guerilla Growing

160 pages $14.95 US
60 full color photos
5 ° x 8 °, illustrated, index
Available in English, German , Spanish.

Marijuana Outdoors: Guerilla Growing is the most current up-to-date source of information on outdoor marijuana growing available. Novice and experienced growers will learn how today's growers are achieving record harvests. Cervantes traveled throughout North America, Europe, Great Britain and Australia to learn how growers harvest the best bud in the world. Instructions and examples from actual growers combined with basic cultivation techniques make this book the most valuable outdoor grow guide a grower could own.

Indoor Marijuana Horticulture

400 pages $21.95 US
5 ° x 8 °, illustrated, index
Available in English, Dutch, German

Indoor Marijuana Horticulture, known as the indoor Bible, continues in its second decade as the best selling indoor marijuana grow guide in the world. This book has everything an indoor grower could want to know about organic and hydroponic gardening, building a grow room, seed selection, cloning, grow lights, growing techniques, problem solving, harvesting and more. Garden calendar and weekly checklist and three case studies are the frosting on the bud!

Marijuana Indoors: Five Easy Gardens

152 pages $14.95 US
60 full color photos
5 ° x 8 °, illustrated, index
Available in English, German , Spanish.

In Marijuana Indoors: Five Easy Gardens five growers tell step-by-step how they grow high-yielding super potent marijuana indoors. Growers explain how to select a house, build a grow room, install ventilation, white walls, hydroponic gardens, high intensity lights, everything they did to grow a super marijuana crop. Growers share detailed cultivation techniques including: varieties to grow, how to clone, water, fertilize, avoid problems, harvest and rotate crops to get the maximum harvest from their rooms.

■■■

Name _____

Address _____

City _____ State _____ Zip _____

Telephone _____

Credit Card # _____ Expiration Date _____

Send Money Orders &   VPP, PO Box 1034
  Credit Card Orders to: Camas, WA 98607

Orders Toll Free: 1-888-989-4800

Questions: 1-360-837-3368
Fax: 1-360-837-3319
Website: http://www.marijuanagrowing.com

Add $4 for Priority Mail, $6 Canada, $10 Europe, $15 Pacific Rim, per book. Orders without postage will be sent Book Rate, and arrive in about 8 weeks. Orders are shipped same day received.